FLORENCE:
the days of the flood

by Franco Nencini

preface by Enrico Mattei

ℑⅅ Stein and Day

Stein and Day/Publishers/7 East 48 Street, New York, N.Y. 10017

Printed in Italy

Contents

How the people of Florence fought back

Dawn, November 5, 1966

I missed ten hours of the drama—the ten hours it took me, that fateful fourth of November, to get from Rome to the Piazza San Marco in Florence. I made the journey with an expedition organised by Minister Pieraccini and Under Secretary Ceccherini in a desperate attempt to force a way through the multiple ring of water that had isolated the Tuscan capital.

"We will try," said Pieraccini. "We will get there somehow or other—and if the worst comes to the worst we can always turn back."

"You are an optimist," I replied. "We might find ourselves cut off in both directions. Some friends of mine were trapped like that on the Via Cassia near Siena this very morning."

His optimism was justified. At six o'clock in the evening, after a seven-hour, detour-ridden journey up the autostrada, we reached our destination. We stopped, or rather we were brought to a halt, high up the Via Cavour, where the waters of the Arno had lost their impetus. Behind a curtain of driving rain pierced here and there by dim, mysterious lights, the Piazza San Marco was like a storm-tossed lake. This lake was fed by a violent torrent which poured down from the Piazza dell'Annunziata, lapped at the church and went swirling off down the Via Cavour in the direction of the Cathedral. Beneath the grim rumbling of the water we could hear a subdued murmur of human voices as people spared by the flood commented on the events of the day. There was no weeping or lamentation. In the people I was able to observe or talk to I found only an anxious concern for those who were down in the flooded part of the city and a sort of stupefied horror. Neither then nor later did I see anyone give way to despair—not even during the unforgettable night we spent on the fringe of that stricken city which, for all its nearness, was now as mysterious and inaccessible as the farthest planet.

On the morning of the fifth the water withdrew from the city centre, leaving behind a noisome deposit of mud and oil. I struggled knee-deep through the slime, slipping and falling more than once, and made my way to the newspaper offices, which it had been impossible to reach the night before. The route I followed was that imposed upon me by the condition of the streets. And in the Borgo Pinti, the Via dei Pilastri, the Piazzetta di Sant'Ambrogio, the mean streets about the Piazza Ghiberti, and the Borgo alla Croce I met the people of Florence for the first time in my life. I thought I had known them before: my mother was a woman of Florence; I had worked long years for the Nuovo Giornale *and* La Nazione; *for ten years I had written a daily column for Florentine readers; and for a further five years I had served them as an editor. But the people I met that morning, young and old alike, seemed to belong to a race of human beings that I had never encountered before. I was walking through a dead city inhabited by living men who were determined to go on living—and determined that their city should live again. The murmuring voices of the previous night were silent now; the people of Florence were at work. They worked with brooms and buckets—and those who had no brooms or buckets had made primitive shovels for themselves out of smashed window-frames, wrecked doors, broken chairs. With these simple tools the people of Florence were attacking the slimy mud that had engulfed the basements and lower floors of their homes and shops. And in the hours to come the new Pompeii would be yielding up the battered remnants of the goods and chattels swallowed by the flood.*

The people of Florence, alone, were beginning the work of salvage. They went about their task in silence, each one doing what he had to do, as if they were all members of one army, commanded by one invisible but omnipresent general. Inspired by their love for Florence, they laboured on—and the most divided and contentious population in the world found unity and brotherhood in the service of the stricken city. Most of those engaged upon that first fierce work of recovery had spent the fateful day in the heart of the city, had personally survived the flood; those who had been outside the worst hit areas, long prevented by the waters from coming in to help, had witnessed only a tiny part of the disaster. And yet, confusedly, instinctively, they all knew that the scenes of ruin and desolation that lay before their own eyes must be matched throughout the city—their city, their beloved Florence, ancient and modern, of craftsmen and small shopkeepers and street traders, the Florence of the Porcellino and the Piazza dei Ciompi. Confusedly and instinctively they knew that their work now—with broom and bucket and homemade shovel—was the first blow struck against the invading enemy, the first manifestation of the city's will to live. Each man fought in his own home, or in his neighbour's home, in his own shop, or in his neighbour's shop, on his own stretch of pavement, or his neighbour's stretch of pavement; but each man knew himself to be just one member of a great and united army fighting for Florence—fighting back!

To me, as I watched and participated in the work, it was a moving and inspiring experience, and I shall always thank Providence for the privilege of having lived through it. It was only late on the following morning, as I sloshed through the mud of Santa Croce and the Via dei Benci in the wake of an imposing presidential tour of inspection, that I heard from certain stricken houses the heart-chilling shouts for "Bread!" and "Water!" This was the first time since the disaster that I had heard anyone speak these words. For forty-eight hours the people of Florence had no thought for themselves; hunger and thirst were as nothing compared with the anguish and heart-ache they endured as they beheld the suffering of their beloved city.

Enrico Mattei

Florence: the flooded areas are shown in grey.

A ton of mud
for every inhabitant

To Our City   *I have faith in the recovery of Florence. Though these have been some of the saddest days in all our history, life has already begun again. The blind man in the Piazza San Marco is back selling his lottery tickets and promising his customers that they will have good fortune. Children are being born. People are getting married. The roses blooming in the flood-ruined garden of the Casa Bargellini have lost something of their earlier symbolical significance. The tragic, heroic days are behind us now. They have left us older and greyer, perhaps, but also stronger—and prouder than we have ever been of our city, conscious of what the world has given us and why it has given it. We have counted our dead, and we shall not forget them. Our account remains open; only a part of it has as yet been presented. And in the meantime—we work.*

There is truth in what Giovanni Spadolini wrote the day after the tragedy: "Florence symbolises the breakdown of mankind in the atomic age—launched as we are upon a proud and unending advance towards progress, well-being and the realisation of the full potentialities of life, scarcely giving a thought to the mystery that dwells within ourselves and all about us, so avid are we for a future rich with the promise of delight... And though man can still remain helpless before the forces of nature, he is able—and indeed it is his inescapable duty—to mitigate their effects. Nor should we forget that it is only at such times of sorrow and disaster that we encounter those high virtues of solidarity and brotherhood which alone give meaning to life and represent a true victory over the forces of darkness and evil."

The city has not yet risen from the crushing blow. But I have faith in the people of Florence. I am one of them. I was with them in their hour of sorrow; I shared their fierce will to live.

I am grateful to my newspaper, which allowed me to follow this experience through to the end.

In writing this book, I wish to do what I can to ensure that these days will not be forgotten, to ensure that Florence will survive if Nature, a hundred years or more from now, should repeat herself. For this time there was no warning. The world came close to losing Florence, of which there could have remained no more than a memory.

I am deeply indebted to my many colleagues, both Italian and foreign, who have written so skilfully and lovingly about Florence in her hour of trial. Their work has been invaluable to me. I am alone to blame for the errors and omissions inevitable in an account written so short a time after the events.

F. N.

9

Armed Forces Day

The troops spent the evening of November 3rd polishing their boots. Already the tanks and vehicles to be used in the parade were gleaming. Finally the soldiers turned in, exhausted after their long hours of work in the rain preparing for Armed Forces Day. In Italy it always rains on November 4th; it is the wettest holiday in the calendar. The banners flapped heavily in the driving wind and rain—and up in the Arno Valley Fate was preparing the tragedy which, in a few hours' time, would fall upon the city of Florence and along all the course of the river to the sea.

In all probability many lives were saved by the fact that November 4th was a holiday. If it had been an ordinary working day, thousands of people would have been caught like rats in a trap—drowned, trampled to death in a panic, killed in a series of nightmarish road accidents as they fled in terror from the rising waves of muddy, oil-fouled water. The full force of the inundation struck Florence in the space of half an hour—as sudden and as unexpected as a cataclysm on the Day of Judgement.

On a normal working day some hundred thousand people commute into the offices, banks and shops in the centre of the city. Five thousand motor-cars are parked in little more than a square kilometre; and the roads were laid out seven hundred years ago.

On the morning of November 4th the flood waters at their height were travelling at sixty kilometres per hour. They swept away motor-cars and trees, burst into churches, penetrated steel-lined strong-rooms, damaged ancient palaces and great works of art. But mercifully few human lives were lost.

If it had not been a holiday, the city could have been turned into one vast cemetery, and in the years to come tourists would have viewed it with those odd feelings, not entirely free from complacency, which we always have when we visit the scenes of man's cruelty or helplessness—Auschwitz, Agadir, Flanders, Skopje. And we would have had no souvenirs to sell them, for the waters would have carried away our souvenirs—as they carried away the body of an old woman, lengths of cloth, pieces of antique furniture, and jewels from the shops on the Ponte Vecchio—right down to the sea at Bocca d'Arno near the old royal estate of San Rossore.

The Night of November 3rd-4th

The cinemas were crowded on the evening of November 3rd, but few indeed of those cinema-goers could have imagined that, in a city of half a million people, in an age which has seen the conquest of space, they themselves were to live through an experience more dramatic and more terrifying than anything they had seen upon the screen.

The Mayor of Florence, Piero Bargellini, retired to bed after an evening spent working in his book-lined study; there would be ceremonies for him to attend the next day. Colonel Nicola Bozzi, the commanding officer of the Carabinieri, was also asleep by midnight. He was roused by a telephone call from the exchange, where they had received several urgent requests for help from places up the Valdarno. The condition of the rivers was apparently getting rather worrying; in the countryside people were driving their beasts to safety and abandoning their cottages. Similar calls were made to the Mayor, the Prefect and the officers of the Civil Engineering Department. At the Levane and La Penna dams in the Valdarno feverish consultations were being held, and from those dams more than two thousand cubic metres of water per second were pouring down towards Florence.

By 2.30 a.m. Figline Valdarno and the road linking it with Incisa were under two metres of water. Completely cut off, together with the few helpers who had managed to reach them, the inhabitants of the village, led by the mayor and councillors, had begun the desperate task of getting everyone to safety. Already part of the village was completely submerged. Out in the country, people had sought safety on the roofs of their houses; they watched the rising waters and shouted for help. But there was no one to hear.

Prefect De Bernart of Florence hastened to the worst hit areas in an Alfa Romeo belonging to the carabinieri.

On the Ponte Vecchio—the tops of whose arches were by this time only about a metre clear of the water—a dozen or so goldsmiths, called to the scene by night watchmen, were carrying their most precious articles to safety.

At about the same time officers of the Civil Engineering Department tersely informed questioners that there was "an exceptional quantity of water". A hydro-meter up river from Florence was registering 6·90 metres—just 45 cm. less than the maximum reached in the floods of recent years.

Already the city drains, which had been constructed back in the days when Tuscany was a grand duchy, were unable to cope with the weight of water. Powerful jets were issuing from the manholes and gushing a metre into the air. Cellars were already flooded along by the river and in the Santa Croce and San Frediano quarters. The first electricity failures were reported as fuses began to blow out.

There were fears for the safety of the aqueduct, and workmen hastened to the scene. One of the men already on night duty was fifty-two-year-old Carlo Maggiorelli from Pozzolatico, a village in the hills to the south of Florence. He had arrived in the pouring rain at eight o'clock, equipped with a thermos of coffee, half a loaf of bread and a packet of cigarettes. It was he who answered the phone when we rang at 3 a.m. to inquire about the situation in the area round the Via Villamagna. "It's a shambles," he replied breathlessly; "everything's going under..." We begged him to leave, but he said he could not abandon the plant for which he was responsible. He died at his post, and his body was recovered two days later in a tunnel choked with mud. He was the first victim and the first hero of the flood.

On the far side of the city, behind the Cascine park, the Mugnone burst its banks and fell upon the race-course. Half an hour previously the custodian, Cesare Neri, had been warned of the danger by a country policeman. Two hundred and seventy racehorses were in peril. Stable-lads, trainers and owners arrived with lorries, and for three desperate hours they worked getting the thoroughbreds to safety. Then the depth of the water prevented any further attempts, and some seventy terror-stricken horses were left to face a hideous death. Days later, when there were fears of an epidemic in the city, flame-throwers were used to destroy their carcasses.

Tragedy had already struck out in the plain. When the waters of the Arno and its many tributaries invaded Osmannoro, which was once a marsh and is now part of the industrial hinterland of Florence, a family of three made a bid for safety, launching themselves on the flood on a large wooden table. The father clung to the lurching raft with one hand, and with the other tightly clasped his three-year-old daughter Marina. In the blinding rain they could see nothing, and the table collided with trees and telegraph-poles. The man lost his grip and went under; he came up choking with mud and the oily water he had swallowed. He was overcome by dizziness and nausea, and fainted across the table. His wife had also been in the water, and she, too, had lost consciousness. The water tore the child from his arms. As the table was swept past an embankment a girl managed to check their progress, and mother and father were saved. When Marina's body was recovered eighteen days later, they were both still in hospital, the father suffering from bronchial pneumonia, the mother in danger of losing her reason.

Dawn   Florence slept as the waters rose. A few early risers were up and away for a morning's shooting—little guessing that there was no countryside left for them to shoot in. The authorities watched over the sleeping city, but they were unable to foresee the future.

It was probably about four o'clock when the mass of water discharged by the Valdarno dams, and the far greater mass pouring down from tributary rivers which had themselves already sown death and destruction, reached the outskirts of the city. It has not yet been established how long it took that terrifying flow of water to reach Florence and overwhelm her. Some authorities say eight hours, some three. Normal reckoning is powerless in the face of such phenomena. But perhaps even three hours would have been enough for people to realise what was happening, enough for them to decide for themselves whether to secure the safety of their most treasured possessions and sit it out, or to flee precipitately and risk a fearful death in their motor-cars.

In the low-lying parts of the city the flood was already sweeping away trees and motor-cars—and still Florence slept. The Lungarno Acciaioli was breached, and a huge mass of water poured over the parapet on the Lungarno alle Grazie. Gas, electricity and water supplies were cut off almost everywhere.

At six in the morning I drove down the Viale dei Colli in the hope of reaching San Frediano and the Ponte Vecchio, which, it was said, could not last much longer. Here and there people were waiting in the darkness for trams that would never come. In the Via Senese, down near the Porta Romana, muddy water was spurting up out of the drains. I turned down the Via Maggio and found water half a metre deep. "Where do you think you're going?" people shouted. "The embankment is giving way at the Ponte Santa Trinita!" In the streets of antique-shops and small craftsmen near the Pitti Palace people were working with torches and candles, racing against time to clear the lower floors of their houses. But dozens of shops and storehouses were already deep in water. A bare-footed old man in a long grey coat wept. "We're done for," he said. Over his shoulders he carried two eighteenth century gilt chairs, damaged irreparably.

There was no hope now of averting the catastrophe. Disaster was overtaking Florence, and the world knew nothing of what was going on. Ninety per cent of her own inhabitants knew nothing. The storm-darkened day broke over the desolate city. Her buildings were beflagged, and her streets were awash with muddy water.

The city's electric clocks came to a standstill at 7.26. The agony of Florence had begun. The Arno flowed over the parapets of the San Niccolò bridge, and the carabinieri blocked the road with an army lorry. The water was two metres deep in the Gavinana district. Then it came over the parapets of the Ponte alle Grazie and the Ponte Vecchio. The city was cut in two and isolated from the rest of the world, unreachable by land, unreachable by air—utterly remote from the seat of government in Rome. There was no electric power, thousands of houses were flooded, and the first victims already lay beneath the mud—the old, the sick and the helpless. From the roofs of low houses in the poorer parts of the city people were crying in vain for help.

When I passed the road-block at the Ponte San Niccolò the roaring of the river was tremendous. The spray off the yellow, ever-spreading river brought visibility down to a minimum. In the city centre the traffic was in a dangerous state of chaos.

At eight o'clock the Comiliter barracks was flooded; the water was rising in the carabinieri barracks in the Borgo Ognissanti. They were hoping that the flood was at its height and that they would soon be able to get out with their vehicles. Half an hour later the engines of those vehicles were under water.

A few hundred metres away in the same street stood the hospital of San Giovanni di Dio. The generator packed up, and the building was plunged in darkness. The basement filled with water, and the first trickles of the flood ran through the wards on the ground floor. By candlelight and torchlight, amid the screams of the suffering, they began the task of transferring two hundred patients to the floors above, aged people among them, and some who had been operated on only a few hours previously. As doctors, nurses and nuns desperately carried their charges up the stairs, the hospital's entire stock of food vanished beneath a cataract of oily, muddy water. In the heart of a flooded city the hospital subsisted for twenty-four hours on ten chickens and twenty bottles of mineral water—the sum total of what had been saved.

A great lake was spreading over the city. At police headquarters it was expected that at any moment the Prefect would give the order for the army to be called in; but in fact the state of emergency was never declared and the military were never given full powers. Florence was now a huge trap from which there was no escape. The road to Bologna was blocked by landslips, the autostrada was cut to north and south, the road to Pisa was under water, and the Via Cassia was completely impassable. In the direction of Siena, too, the news was bad.

The embankments were now merely a part of the river. The water was pouring down towards the Via Tripoli, the Via delle Casine, the Via Ghibellina and the Via dell'Agnolo, and the whole of the area round the Via dei Bardi was about to go under. The Ponte Vecchio was still holding out against the incredible violence of the flood. The river had completely burst its banks, sweeping away parapets and trees and tearing the very stones out of the roads; hundreds of metres of embankment were broken down on the Lungarno Ferrucci, the Lungarno Serristori and the Lungarno delle Grazie. The rising waters carried away hundreds of motor-cars, flinging them violently against walls, doors and street-signs.

The situation in the Gavinana district was desperate. The flood had already claimed four victims among the aged and defenceless in that quarter alone: Armido Peruzzi (71), who was drowned, probably in his sleep, in a basement in the Via di Rusciano; Pietro and Giuseppina Cocchi (74 and 52), determined to cling to their home to the last; and Ermenegildo Livi (81), who simply had not the strength to struggle against the waters.

By nine o'clock, at least 20,000 people were in the grip of personal tragedy—those who had gone out early in the morning and were now cut off, knowing their homes and loved ones to be in danger. Hundreds of cars had forced the road-block at the Ponte San Niccolò and were climbing for safety up towards the Piazzale Michelangiolo. From them, and from the hundreds of cars down in the town whose electrical circuits had been completed by the water, there rose a dreary wailing of horns. This mournful sound was the day-long accompaniment to the flood—together with the shouts of those who were trapped, the barking of dogs, the pounding of the water against the walls of buildings two or even three metres above the ground, and the hollow rumbling of exploding boilers.

Shortly after nine it was impossible for traffic in the Piazza del Duomo to turn in the direction of the Arno. The Piazza della Signoria was still dry, but the cross streets were almost a metre deep in muddy water. At 9.45 a.m. the flood burst into the Piazza del Duomo.

In all parts of the affected area the water was filling cellars and damaging central heating oil-tanks, and before long vast quantities of black and greasy oil had joined the flow of mud and water. It was this oil which later bore witness to the magnitude of the flood, tracing a black tidemark across the façades of buildings. It was this oil which wrought havoc among books and works of art, penetrated to the most secret parts of intricate machinery, and brought humiliation to the greatest achievements of human ingenuity.

The Fight
And yet, dazed and desperate as they were, the people of Florence drew strength from the age-old love they bore for their city, which belonged not to them alone but to the whole world, and fought back against the invading river. At dawn on that ill-fated Friday, when both the past and the future of Florence were threatened, there were those who rallied to her defence: Ugo Procacci, the Superintendent of Fine Art, Father Cocci of Santa Croce, Umberto Baldini, chief of the restoration department, Luisa Becherucci, head of the Uffizi—and many more besides, policemen, monks, workmen, less well-known perhaps, but all inspired by the same high sense of purpose.

Here is Luisa Becherucci's story as published in *L'Europeo*:

"Shortly after seven o'clock I was informed by telephone that the Arno had overflowed and that the Via della Ninna was flooded. I telephoned at once to Superintendent Procacci and rushed here. We arrived here in ones and twos just after eight—about the time that the water was reaching the Piazza della Signoria. Baldini, the head of the restoration department, also came; he was soaked to the skin, so he went and took his clothes off and wrapped himself in a couple of blankets. With us and a few members of the museum staff, there were about a dozen people altogether. At ten o'clock the telephone went dead, and we were isolated. Through a passage on the third floor we were still in communication with the Palazzo Vecchio, where Mayor Bargellini and about forty other people were marooned. We got ourselves organised at once and began rescue operations, working from the bottom of the building upwards. We carried everything to safety from the restoration rooms in the Vecchia Posta, but it was impossible to get into those in the Via della Ninna. We rescued some works of great importance—Filippo Lippi's "Incoronazione", Masaccio's "Madonna di San Giovenale", two Simone Martinis from the Berenson collection and Giotto's great Badia polyptych, all of which were in the Uffizi for restoration. We took the collection of portraits from the Corridoio degli Archibusieri and carried up from the mezzanine floor some three hundred pictures which had been stacked there to await cleaning. Botticelli's "Incoronazione" was one of these. Throughout the morning and the afternoon, so long as the light lasted, we kept it up, dealing with the pictures, as far as possible, in their order of importance."

Maria Luisa Bonelli, the curator of the Museo della Scienza, was alone. She woke at dawn to find that there was already half a metre of water. She dressed hastily and began carrying upstairs the exhibits displayed in the ground-floor rooms—the Edison phonograph, articles from the Grand Duke Pietro Leopoldo's pharmacy, the wonders of eighteenth century science. But the waters continued to rise, and the first floor also was threatened. "Then I took my courage in both hands. I got out of a second-floor window, went along a cornice and smashed a window into the State Archives. The water was still rising, so I carried away some exhibits of exceptional historical value, such as Galileo's telescope."

Father Gustavo Cocci, Franciscan and historian, of Santa Croce was just leaving to say Mass in another church when he found his way barred by the water. It was already up to the door-handles of the cars parked in the piazza. Shortly afterwards it rose still more and forced its way into one of the finest and most famous churches in Italy.

The monks, according to Guido Gerosa writing in *Epoca*, were terrified. As soon as the water permitted they struggled down the naves and went to see what had happened in the Cappella dei Pazzi. Using tables as rafts, they pushed on to the cloisters by Arnolfo di Cambio and Brunelleschi, where they were met by a scene of absolute desolation. Large, dark-coloured bundles were bobbing about on the swirling waters. These were documents and manuscripts which had floated through a smashed doorway from the neighbouring Biblioteca Nazionale. Beyond that door the riches of the great library lay victims of the flood: 24,000 manuscripts, 705,000 letters and documents, 3,800 incunabula, 3,000,000 volumes and opuscules, 68,000 musical works. The monks tried in vain to open the door to the crypt; the altar-step had moved and was blocking the way. In the old refectory, which now houses the museum, the water had completely covered a magnificent "Crucifixion". This was Cimabue's masterpiece, "which marks the transition from mediaeval art to the world of Giotto. It was seventy per cent destroyed, and was the greatest single artistic loss suffered during the flood. For two days monks and restoration experts went through the mud and water left behind by the inundation, recovering one by one the minute fragments of colour that had been flaked off by the water..."

14

Meanwhile the flow of water, mud and oil, powerful enough to bear the trunks of uprooted trees, had reached the Baptistery in the Piazza del Duomo. One after the other five panels were torn from the Porta del Paradiso: "Creation of Adam and Eve", "Original Sin", "Cain and Abel", "The Story of Esau", "Jacob and Joseph". Two panels also fell from Andrea Pisano's south door. A thick layer of mud settled over these precious works of art, but fortunately their weight and the protective gates prevented them from being swept away. They were rescued the following day.

At eleven o'clock the B.B.C. broadcast an alarm from London: "The world is losing one of its most precious jewels—the city of Florence." New York television began transmitting bulletins on the state of things in the Tuscan capital.

And all the time the fight went on to save human lives and works of art. At the convent of San Marco the works of Fra Angelico were preserved for posterity; and out in the parish of San Donnino a priest in a yellow rowing-boat accompanied the funeral of a woman who had been drowned in the flood. Wherever and whenever it was possible the people of Florence fought to defend their history and their dignity against the evil rising tide of disaster.

Cut Off

Like so many others, I, too, was cut off—for twenty-four hours. After the terrible night and the tragic dawn I returned to the newspaper offices at about nine o'clock on the Friday morning and, with the harrowing scenes of the catastrophe still fresh in my mind, began to write my report for a special edition of the paper—which was in fact fated never to appear. There were about twenty of us in all in the *Nazione* building, which had been inaugurated only a month previously and contained some of the most advanced equipment in Europe. I thought I had better telephone my wife, who was at home about a kilometre away, to let her know what was going on. It took me half an hour to get through to her—and then I had the impression that she thought I must be exaggerating. By ten o'clock the building was surrounded by a metre and a half of water; and the level was rising fast. We had tried to make a sortie in the cars, but even before we reached the road it was obvious that any such attempt would be the height of folly. By eleven o'clock the great room containing the rotary presses was completely under water, and only the roofs of our cars could be seen.

All around us the tragedy was being acted out. In every street, in every house, there were the same conflicting elements of hope, anguish, solidarity, violence, rage and incredulity.

A number of guard dogs were still shut up in the warehouses of the old market of Sant'Ambrogio; they howled desperately until at last the waters closed over them. People were climbing onto the roofs of the poor, single-storey houses near the *Nazione* offices, waving bed-sheets in the air to attract attention to themselves. They were in need, and we were powerless to help them. Shortly after this a tank arrived outside the walls of the prison nearby, its lights absurdly glowing in the daylight. Word went round that a massive escape bid was under way and that the warders were being overwhelmed. We learnt later that at that moment prisoners were being transferred, amid scenes of indescribable confusion, to the third floor of the gaol.

At 11·30 there was a violent explosion from the direction of the Piazza Beccaria, followed by a grim column of black smoke. It was probably a store of paraffin going up. The people on the roofs of the houses near the office began shouting for help. In a little single-storey house just opposite the type-setting room we could see four pale faces staring out from behind the curtains at the inexorably rising waters. Still it rained. Lorries parked in the piazza had completely disappeared beneath the flood; so had our presses. Huge rolls of newsprint, each one weighing several tons, had been swept out of the warehouses and were wallowing about in the roadway.

Troops and firemen had been at work for hours already on the outskirts of

15

the flooded area, but there was little they could do in the central zone as yet. The current was racing along at about sixty kilometres per hour, and the amphibious vehicles of the fire service were being swept out of control and thrown dangerously against the walls of buildings. The units concerned gave proof of the highest gallantry, but they were able to make only desperate and isolated rescue attempts.

Half the city now lay at the mercy of the flood. The other half had no idea of the gravity of the events taking place. At an old people's home run by nuns in the Via Masaccio a blind and half paralysed old lady named Italia Borgogni was trapped in her room. Last-minute attempts to save her were unsuccessful, and she drowned. We heard later that, at the far end of that same Via Masaccio, beyond the railway bridge, people were quietly sitting in the Aurora cinema watching a film starring Sean Connery.

About three o'clock there was another tremendous explosion, this time in the Via Scipione Ammirato, as tanks of carbide were flung violently together in a particularly oily stretch of water. For many minutes the smoke hung heavy in the sky. People in houses nearby were thrown about by the blast, and an eighty-four-year-old pensioner was left hanging lifeless from the shattered roof of the building in which the explosion occurred. His wife and seven other people, including the well-known singer Paolo Washington, were injured—and with two metres of water in the street it was impossible for them to leave the building in search of help. From window to window and roof-top to roof-top their call for help was passed finally to the headquarters of the fire service a kilometre and a half away, and an hour later a squad of men reached them, at the risk of their own lives, by boat.

Once more we heard firing from the Santa Teresa prison. "It's a mutiny!" people were shouting from their roofs. The terror which for some hours had been growing among the prisoners (the water in the gaol was almost four metres deep) had now exploded into violence among the two hundred-odd men who had been transferred to the top floor. The warders had been overpowered, and about eighty prisoners had made their way out onto the roofs, from where they were diving down into the muddy, oil-fouled waters below. The bolder ones made good their escape, but one of the youngest among them hesitated, poised on the edge of the roof. From the nearby houses people shouted encouragement: "Go on, jump! There's a tree-trunk just coming!" A woman yelled: "Where do you think you're going?" He was screwing up his courage. "I'm going to Montecatini," he shouted back, "to take the waters!" He dived for the tree-trunk—and missed. He struggled desperately before the foul waters closed above his head. His name was Luciano Sonnellini, and the water to which he had turned for freedom carried his body more than a kilometre from the gaol. It was recovered days later in a cellar in the Via dei Pepi.

In the hospitals conditions were chaotic. The flood reached the San Salvi mental hospital shortly after midday, invading the grounds and tearing up paving-stones as if they were made of paper. Within an hour the water was three metres deep. Some of the patients howled with terror; others were silent and as if petrified. The staff tried to comfort them, speaking quietly and soothingly, as one would speak to a frightened child, but there was despair in their hearts, for they knew that the pharmacy had been flooded and that the drugs which might have been used to calm the patients during the night to come had all been lost. But while the patients were being evacuated from the flooded parts of the hospital, two of the staff managed to make their way to a nearby embankment, along which they were able to run in search of help. Before nightfall men of the fire service brought in a boatload of medical supplies.

At the Meyer children's hospital the electricity had failed, and about sixty babies in incubators were in danger of their lives. The parents wept or paced the floor in desperation, but some of the more enterprising spirits went to scour the dry part of the city for generators. They found them in the Piazza Indipendenza displayed on a stand set up as part of the celebrations for Armed Forces Day—and the babies' lives were saved.

At Montedomini the waters were rising to threaten the lives of a thousand old people. The huge ground-floor rooms of the sad-looking building in the Via Malcontenti were occupied by the bed-ridden, the blind and the children's department. All of these had to be got to safety. The blind linked hands and formed a chain; the old and helpless were carried bodily up the stairs. The whole lot were saved by six attendants and one inspector.

"Imagine that you are eighty years old and that your home is being flooded," wrote Pier Francesco Listri. "At Montedomini a thousand old folk waited helplessly as the waters rose. Some of them were unable to grasp the significance of what was happening. I saw one old man in a skull-cap and striped trousers solemnly trying to sweep the water out of the courtyard with a broom... Most of the inmates were a prey to mental confusion. Either they did nothing, or they devoted their energies to trifles. There were old ladies worried about the dampness of the landing—when the whole ground floor was awash with water; others searching for a cat, or a particular bed-sheet marked with their name. It is not easy to understand what is happening, or to fight against it, when you are eighty years old and your home is flooded."

The battle for Florence was on. And life was continuing. There were births and deaths. Twelve children were born at Careggi on November 3rd, nine of them during the period when the city was under water. The dead lying in their coffins awaiting burial in the funeral chapel of Sant'Egidio were rescued from the flood.

Marooned in our splendid modern building, surrounded by four metres of water, we lost all idea of time, all power of thought. We were able to take in only what was going on around us. We had found a transistor radio, and, though the battery soon ran out, we had had some brief contact with the outside world. At the time it seemed like a first promise of salvation. Amid the atmospherics we heard the confident voice of the news-reader: "The country is celebrating Armed Forces Day. President Moro has visited..." Towards the end of the bulletin there was news of the bad weather conditions affecting central Italy. Flooding was reported from Florence...

Another boat went by, perilously driven by the current. It had stopped raining. We decided to do what we could before nightfall to rescue the family in the house opposite, making use of a little boat we had on the premises. Securing it with ropes, we somehow got it across the road and tied up to their window. The family was made up of father, mother, a girl of twelve called Simonetta, and a baby of two, Roberto, who was sucking a dummy which seemed in imminent danger of falling into the water. The father was the first one to scramble down the ladder into the boat. The ten metres of the roadway seemed like an ocean; the flood had swallowed up lorries, houses, factories—and those struggling human figures looked very small and frail. Somehow the operation was completed—just as it was getting dark.

In the stricken area south of the river people were beginning by this time to hazard themselves out of doors. Here is an account by the Florentine writer Carlo Coccioli, as published in the newspaper *Il Giorno*.

"I went out about four o'clock in the afternoon. It was not easy as the entrance-hall was covered with a thick layer of oily mud which seemed to stretch right across the street. I went back upstairs for a walking-stick, then came down again and probed the noisome lake that seemed to be cutting me off from the rest of the world. It was about eighty centimetres deep. Slowly I advanced through it. I started across the Piazza Pitti in the direction of the Via Guicciardini, but I was soon brought to a halt. The Via dello Sprone, the Via dei Ramaglianti, the Via Toscanella and, farther off, the Borgo San Jacopo were a maze of turgid, oil-blackened torrents. The water had uprooted the newsagent's kiosk at the corner of the Ponte Vecchio. Though it was getting dark, I thought I could see the bridge almost completely under water. In its tumultuous flow the water was carrying motor-cars, chests of drawers, chairs, doors and window-frames, viciously flinging these things into heaps against walls and at street-corners. And always, obstinately obedient to the law of nature, the water sought and found for itself a path through those aged buildings that was downhill and roughly parallel to the course of the river...

"I drove up to the Piazzale Michelangiolo. Before me and behind me were long lines of cars. There was a small crowd of people in the piazzale, looking down at the city. Night had fallen by now, and there were no lights to be seen; it rained incessantly, and Florence lay at the mercy of her enraged river. There was no voice offering counsel, not a searchlight, no bells ringing, no help being given—only silence. Talkative, argumentative and sarcastic though they normally are, the people of Florence were playing out their drama in silence. The river alone was heard; there was nothing but the river, with its swirling admixture of oil and mud. I came down the hill once more, parked the car and walked along the Via Romana. It was so dark that pedestrians were making short guttural sounds to warn others of their approach. Wrapped in darkness, more guessed at than actually seen, the Pitti Palace stood massive and magnificent. For the first time since the day it was built it could be called beautiful. Back in the eighty centimetres of mud, I returned home, groping my way in pitch darkness up to my flat on the seventh floor. My first urge was to weep for Florence—but then my mind filled with thoughts of God. I flung myself on my bed, lit a candle and opened the Bible. I thought of God and, though I had no idea of the extent of the flood, it suddenly made sense that the full force of the disaster should have fallen on the proud heart of our city—with its rich merchants and thriving goldsmiths, with its middle-men buying the products of craftsmen and selling them to American tourists for four times as much—and for a moment it seemed to me that I had almost understood this manifestation of God's wrath. But then I thought of those small craftsmen and their obscure devastated workshops, of their hungry children, and the simple delights of those whose idea of heaven is a motor-scooter, a television set, a meal of dried cod on Fridays, an occasional visit to a football match... In my imagination I saw the coarsened hands and watery eyes of their womenfolk and I sensed the fierceness of their daily struggle to keep going in a world becoming ever more inhuman. And, at the thought of the suffering inflicted upon the lives of those humble folk, my supposed understanding of God's will evaporated. But in the Book of Job I sought the passage where the Lord replies obliquely to the insistent questioning of the man smitten by fate. 'Who,' He asks—thought not perhaps in so many words—'who made the hippopotamus and the crocodile, you or God?' and: 'Who is this that darkeneth counsel by words without knowledge?' And having read these words, I fell asleep."

The Longest Night Only a small proportion of the people in the affected parts of the city were able to leave their houses with the coming of evening. A hundred thousand people were still marooned in the upper parts of houses or on the roofs. It was a fearful night that now settled over the devastated city.

We thought we heard more firing from the direction of the prison.

At least, though, the water was not rising so fast now. And finally, from out of the lurid sunset sky, like an explosion of hope, there came the distant roaring of a helicopter. This was the first really effective help there had been. Previous rescue attempts, made by rubber dinghies, amphibians and light tanks, had made only a slight difference to the overall picture. But now, every five

18

or six minutes, the helicopter was coming in and lifting groups of shocked and mud-caked people off the roof-tops. One old lady fell to her death during one of these operations. From Bellariva and the south bank of the river the helicopter lifted off women and children and old people who had known the same heart-break and suffering experienced by their ancestors in the floods of centuries gone by. The rescued were taken to the Campo di Marte, where hundreds of people from the dry parts of the city had gathered to render comfort and assistance.

The flood and the failure of communications had split the city in two, but the solidarity of the population now asserted itself. Those who had been spared the tragedy began to understand what had happened, piece the story together from the confused words and staring eyes of the refugees. All who were able to opened their homes to their less fortunate fellow-citizens.

With the coming of darkness the rescue operations ceased. Every so often distress rockets went off against the blackness of the sky; but these appeals for help remained unanswered. The wind got up, and all at once, incredibly, the clouds parted and a first star appeared. We could see the headlights of cars climbing up to the Piazzale Michelangiolo—but from the flood area there still came cries for help and the frenzied barking of dogs at large upon the roof-tops.

Suddenly a workman burst into the type-setting room, where we were preparing for a siege. "It's going down!" he shouted. We went down with a torch to measure the water. It was just five metres deep. We made a mark on the stairs, and when we went back an hour later the water had in fact fallen by twelve centimetres; by nine o'clock it had gone down almost a metre. We felt free at last, as we had felt years before at the end of the war—and as tired as if all the mud and water in the world had passed over us. Chairs were banging into one another as they floated about in the conference room, and it was ac-companied by this sound that we settled down for the longest night we had ever known.

The Escapers   About 1 a.m. a fine rain began to fall.

"Strange, mud-caked figures came towards us, their faces distorted with terror," wrote Piero Magi. "No one knew which way to go. The only thing that mattered was to get out of the danger area. A lot of people had brought their cars right up to the edge of the flood waters—sightseers. The radio had asked people to keep off the roads if they possibly could; but to us those headlights were a symbol of hope. There were still shouts coming from the worst threatened houses. Every now and then we came across military units or men of the fire service, but the water remained a well-nigh impassable obstacle. Ragged people covered in mud from head to foot appeared at the roadside. With them we exchanged news, but the only thing we were sure of was that we were still alive. From the parts of the city that had been spared people came running in hundreds, scarcely able to credit what had occurred. They formed themselves into teams of volunteeers as a cold wind got up and moved like a shudder across the surface of the flooded city."

The waters continued to subside, and hundreds of silent, hunched figures appeared at the side of the river, hoping to get across. There were still many hours of waiting ahead of them. Some had loved ones on the other side; some had shops to worry about, or motor-cars; some, who were free of such anxieties, had come simply to offer help. With lamps and torches in their hands they waited.

The men who had escaped from prison went their various ways. One group of dangerous characters robbed a gunsmith's shop, stole a boat and managed to cover their tracks. Another group gave themselves up, returned to the gaol and later played a worthy part in rescue operations. Others, who had made their escape across the roof-tops, reached the institute of the Dominican nuns in the Via Manzoni. They knocked on the skylight and demanded food and water. They promised not to do anyone any harm, but the nuns played for time so successfully that at last, the water-level having noticeably subsided, most of the men decided to try their luck on the ground. Some of them still thought the best thing to do was to try and get into a house, however, and before long Signor Arnaldo Lumachini, who lived in that same Via Manzoni, saw a group of men advancing cautiously across the roof of the neighbouring house.

"I opened the window that gave onto the terrace," he later told a reporter from *L'Europeo*. "The gaol-breakers came indoors. They were unkempt, shivering with cold and soaked to the skin. There were men of all shapes and sizes. Some of them looked pretty tough customers; and some just looked desperately unhappy. But the odd thing was they all seemed shy and embarrassed. At last a tall, swarthy young fellow with a soaking wet scarf wound round his neck cleared his throat. 'We don't mean anyone any harm,' he said; 'we just want to get down to the street. Up at the prison they gave the order every man for himself, and we came over the roofs...' "

Another one of them confirmed that they merely wanted to reach the street—but the street was three metres deep in water. The night that followed was fantastic, like a dream. The men were all on their best behaviour, exchanging polite remarks, offering cigarettes—and never failing to use the ashtrays. They courteously accepted food from their startled hosts. Perhaps what they had needed most of all was the warmth of human companionship. A man who was serving a term for robbery spoke to Lumachini's sister. "Signora, as soon as I'm in a position to do somebody a good turn I'll remember you and your family."

When morning came they helped to tidy the house and then swam off down the street.

Very few people slept that night. Everywhere people were awake—in the hospitals amid the groans of the suffering, on the roof-tops fighting against exhaustion, in the flooded and devastated houses of Gavinana, and in the top floors of the buildings along the river. And all that night fearful news somehow managed to circulate among the flooded streets. There were tales of people being trapped and drowned in the subways at the railway station, where the waters had brought the gates crashing down, irrevocably shut; there were reports of broken dams and entire towns being wiped out in the Valdarno. Nothing seemed beyond the bounds of possibility. Every hour we went and checked the water level, which continued to fall. In barracks about the town the troops were preparing for the work that lay ahead. Feverish high-level consultations were taking place. Preparations were being made for a new era in the history of Florence: "After the Flood".

First Light
About six in the morning, with the coming of daylight, the ravaged city could be seen rising from a sea of mud. Hundreds of houses were half buried in the stuff.

There was a dead man just outside the newspaper building, his oil-blackened arm protruding from beneath a Fiat 1500. An ambulance and an Alfa Romeo were standing by. A carabiniere came up and spoke to me quietly. "Move along, sir, if you please. There's a woman here crying, and we think it might be her husband. Move along, please."

The people were coming out into the streets, wading through the mud, silently and with dignity. With absurdly inadequate tools they began the work of salvage.

And what sadness there was in their eyes! "They began work at once," wrote Arrigo Benedetti, "without waiting for help from the government or the municipal authorities. Independent as ever, they were if anything stimulated by the sluggish reaction of the bureaucrats, and went to work with genuine dedication, just as they had done in 1944 when the war swept over their city... The proprietors of smart dress-shops and their sophisticated sales-ladies scrabbled in the mud. It was as if centuries had passed overnight and the proud materialistic civilisation of which Florence was one of the key centres had come to an end; as if a crisis had shaken the world and emphasised the dreariness of our decadent way of life. It was hard to believe that there even existed an enlightened world in which people were able to enjoy a measure of comfort and well-being..."

I walked home. The nineteenth-century Piazza d'Azeglio and the English Cemetery had been devastated, desecrated, by the flood. Quiet middle-class homes had been laid waste, and there were armed soldiers at the street-corners. Behind lay the desperate chaos of the poorer streets around the Sant'Ambrogio market. An ambulance went by with its siren wailing. I started to run. It was just after seven o'clock. All was silent at home. I found the stubs of candles, a bottle of water, an empty biscuit tin. Everyone was asleep. There was a hint of warmth in the air. Without rousing anyone, I stretched out on my bed and gave thanks to God. Through the shutters came a first shaft of sunlight.

The Cross and the Hammer and Sickle

In those first two terrible days after the flood there was fear abroad in the city. Fear of an epidemic carried on the death-tainted air; fear of escaped prisoners who had stolen weapons and might still be at large in the city; fear of explosions; fear of houses collapsing. There was severe shortage of bread, water and medical supplies. Old folk were dying of pneumonia. At San Donnino and San Mauro out in the countryside many people were still on their roofs, feverishly clutching at the tiles with bloodless hands, still wondering if help would come in time.

In that period when the state was slowly preparing itself for action the people of Florence began, with stoicism and resignation, to free themselves from that suffocating layer of mud. One morning I saw an old man laboriously shovelling up the mud outside his house. His movements were slow and oddly deliberate, and I realised that he was blind. I spoke to him and asked his name. "No!" he answered, recoiling, "I don't want you putting my name in your newspaper; I'm no different from all the others..."

The "others" that he referred to were people who had learnt over the centuries that no one ever does anything for nothing; people who accepted the truth of the proverb "it's an ill wind that blows nobody any good"; lean, ill-starred people who kept themselves going with oaths and sarcasm—but who were capable nevertheless of dying in the defence of their homes and shops. One who died was fifty-one-year-old Mario Filli. On the Sunday, he crossed the city on foot to go and help clear the mud out of his sister's shop at Gavinana. No football for him that Sunday, no cinema or television to celebrate the dawning of hope. After working for fourteen solid hours, he died. His heart gave out. He died of exhaustion, but perhaps it would not be too far from the truth to suggest that a contributory cause was a broken heart—for that is the phrase traditionally used to describe the sorrow and helplessness we experience when overwhelmed by a disaster immeasurably too great for us to cope with.

The flood certainly overwhelmed us—but not us alone. The state itself failed to measure up to the challenge—for all the wealth at its disposal and for all the breath it expended on rhetorical pronouncements. And the deaths of Mario Filli and others, who were overcome by exhaustion or by fumes left lingering in cellars, remain as silent and moving evidence of the courage shown by thousands of Florentines, rich and poor, in humble homes and shops and in the splendid, internationally known establishments of the Via Tornabuoni.

With each family concentrating on its own particular problems, but ever ready to give a helping hand to a neighbour, those Florentines were symbols of the faith which we all have in the future. Three days after the flood one shopkeeper was displaying a sign which read: "New Pompeii Stores—all goods fresh from the mud". While out in the country there were still signs on the roofs reading: "Expectant Mother", "Sick Person" or simply "Water".

21

In San Frediano a workman proudly answered an inquiry from the Duke of Aosta (who, together with ex-King Umberto, was playing a worthy part in the relief work) with the words: "It would take more than a flood to finish off San Frediano!"

And we must not forget the priests. There was one in San Niccolò who somehow managed to get hold of a mechanical digger—this was before the authorities had begun to act—and manoeuvre it up the Via dei Bardi. (The Via dei Bardi, which retained its nobility even in spite of its cruelly damaged houses and its paralysingly thick layers of rubble and mud). And there was a priest from another parish who, after searching night and day for food for his flock, went and denounced six families that had been ruthless enough to buy up vast quantities of foodstuffs and hoard them in their homes.

On November 4th another priest, aided by a group of young men, made valiant efforts to rescue a paralysed old lady trapped by the flood. The attempt failed, so the priest secured a boat, from which he administered extreme unction to the dying woman and prayed with her through her last agony. And throughout the desperate period before help began to flow into the city this same priest went from window to window bringing comfort and distributing all he had to the suffering.

And always, humbly dressed and going about incognito in boats or on the turrets of tanks, there was that old prince of the Church, Monsignor Florit.

And then there were the Communists. Communism is part of the very fabric of working-class life in Tuscany, and the Communists were among the first to take action. They organised distributions of food, water and medical supplies, arranged accomodation for the homeless, and played a valuable part throughout the emergency period. As always, the poor helped the poor—without delay, with or without the blessing of officialdom.

Priests, Communists, carabinieri, troops—these were united in the great work, sometimes risking their lives, chronically short of food and sleep.

It matters not that the events of this period may one day be turned (in some cases have already been turned) to political advantage—whether by bureaucrats jockeying for a place in the presidential party, or by ministers and under secretaries and even smaller fry, regardless of their political colour, only too anxious to be in the public eye. The flood's profit and loss account will probably never be made up, and the sincerity or otherwise of some of the people involved will never be determined. For the moment, at least, we need not worry about such things. Suffice it to say that each one of us retains memories capable of inspiring admiration, disgust, pity and rage.

The Sixth Day

On the sixth day mechanical monsters appeared in all parts of the stricken city The state began to create order out of chaos, and machinery, technicians, engineers, troops, lorries, tanks and boats were all forthcoming. For six days we had been trying to make our position clear. "The telephone calls went out from the Palazzo Vecchio, the Palazzo Medici Riccardi and the Comiliter H.Q.," wrote Nello Ajello, "and the urgent tones of the local authorities echoed meaninglessly about the government offices in Rome. 'The city is under two, even three, metres of mud; there is no food, no drinking water, no accomodation for the homeless, no medical supplies; museums, churches and libraries are filled with vast pools of stagnant water. What are we supposed to do about it?' The first reaction from Rome seemed to be one of mild irritation."

It was hard to get it across that there were 600,000 tons of mud, filth and rubble smothering a city that was at once a huge modern centre and a treasure-house of great art—that artistic masterpieces were going to ruin in a city where there were 15,000 wrecked motor-cars, 5,000 homeless families, a food shortage, and 6,000 shops out of business.

Saragat came and saw. Ministers came and saw. But it took the arrival of a general like De Lorenzo to get things moving; it took an open letter from Enrico Mattei to the President of the Republic. And there are some, even of opposing political views, who believe that the editor of *La Nazione* saved Florence with that letter.

"Mr President, You must know that nothing has changed in that scene of desolation which you visited three days ago. There are some pumps in action, but almost all of them have been brought in from the countryside by private citizens; smashed furniture, doors, windows, rags that were once clothes have been heaped up at the shattered gateways; here and there a stretch of pavement has been cleared of mud. But the task of cleaning up the city is virtually at a standstill. The citizens are complaining at the lack of outside help; few soldiers have been seen in our streets and squares; on our long tour of the city we saw a ludicrously inadequate number of machines at work—and many of these were being operated by private citizens... Situations like the one now existing in our city cannot be dealt with by ordinary administrative methods... Men and women who deserve the highest praise for the courage, calm and pride they have shown in this emergency trust that you, Mr President, will stimulate in the authorities that activity which rulers must show at times of national need if they are to be worthy of their position..."

Until that sixth day the devastated city kept going thanks to the heroism of the troops, the fire and ambulance services, the police, the priests, the Communists and countless others who were prepared to go without food and sleep and hazard both their lives and their popularity.

Before the coming of that sixth day I had already spent many hours wading through the foul, evil-smelling residue that the flood had left in Florence. The people were working, desperately, for hours on end. They felt themselves to be alone; they were ill-equipped; they were haunted by feelings of helplessness. Their sentiments found expression in the cry with which an old woman greeted us in the Via Niccolò da Uzzano. She swept down upon us—"Give us gas, not water! If they gave us gas we could blow ourselves up and put an end to all this! We are alone, and for three days we have been scraping away at this mountain of mud with our hands! Better be dead than go on like this!" Her eyes were red with weeping—and these were the first words of despair that I had heard in all the kilometres I had walked through the worst damaged areas of the city.

Again before that sixth day I had seen death reflected in the eyes of a thirty-year-old man. For eighty hours he had been clinging precariously to a roof on which we touched down in our helicopter. In all that time he had eaten and drunk nothing—and a metre below him lay a sea of mud and water ready to swallow him up if his hands for a moment relaxed their grip. From other roofs nearby, but separated from us by the water, two boys, an old man and two women were calling: "Us, too! Take us, too!" But it was impossible to reach them. There were wires and television aerials hemming them round—the helicopter blades only had to touch one of them and it would have been the end for all of us. An officer lowered himself from the helicopter and threw them bread, water and milk. In his eagerness, and without thinking, he even dropped them some tins of food. And the man, though at the limit of his strength, realised that he must somehow get a share of that food to the others. After eighty hours without food, and before taking a bite for himself, he began crawling along the roof towards them. They were weeping, blowing kisses to the pilot, waving handkerchiefs; exhausted perhaps, but not now entirely without hope.

We will let Alfonso Madeo, the special correspondent of the *Corriere della Sera*, have the last word on those first days following the flood:

"Commune and Prefecture several times tried to elbow each other out of the way. In military circles there was ill-feeling at all levels because the politicians had tried to make capital out of the results achieved by the first courageous relief operations carried out by the troops. The various public bodies acted each within its own sphere, with little attempt at coordination. All were concerned to preserve their own autonomy and initiative, in the hope of getting the credit for having saved Florence. Ministers imposed their will upon the local authorities—and conflict broke out between the various ministries... Individual men, who gave themselves wholeheartedly, were not to blame. It was the fault of the system."

A City which belongs to All the World

I met La Pira one evening in the hospital in the Via Venezia. He was wearing the same grey overcoat I remembered from my university days, and he had the same unshakable faith in humanity. That faith was now vindicated, for help was coming from all parts of the world in response to the telegrams he had sent. "This is what a recovery should be like—anybody and everybody making a contribution. Florence at the moment is a wonderful new experiment; there are parish priests and Communists working side by side on the local committees..." He had just been to one such committee meeting, in Santa Croce, and we asked him how things were going. "Badly," he replied; "the mud seems indestructible—like evil. But man can overcome it if he has faith. And Florence is an expression of faith, a great spiritual reality. The very thought of her being destroyed fills us with dismay—but she is going to recover. And all the world is helping; Russia is sending plane-loads of supplies, and the United States is doing so much..." And with that he went off down the corridor to ask a nun about a telephone call he was putting through to Rabat.

La Pira's presence in the city was little publicised, but was of inestimable value to Florence in her hour of need. So was that of Carlo Ludovico Ragghianti. From his study in the Palazzo Strozzi, above the flood-wrecked Vieusseux library, he sent telegrams to all parts of the world on behalf of his international committee formed to speed the restoration of damaged works of art. And help came from all over the world. Experts came to help with restoration work; students laboured fourteen hours a day in the mud to salvage books in the Biblioteca Nazionale. Innumerable subscription lists were opened, and great sums of money collected. From Aberfan came the toys and clothes of a generation of children who had lost their lives in the landslide.

Nine babies were born amid scenes of chaos and horror on the night of the flood. One ten-day-old baby, Claudia Querci, was thrown into the water with her mother when their house collapsed following a gas explosion. For two hours, with arms outstretched, her mother held her clear of the water. Her aunt, who had been injured in the explosion, managed to come to their assistance at the last moment.

But where were the children of Florence? Some of us wondered in those terrible days when we were threatened by an epidemic, and the stench of decay had us going about the streets with white masks over our mouths. I remember seeing three children from a distance some twenty-four hours after Florence had resumed contact with the outside world. I was driving down the Viale dei Colli towards San Frediano, and they were playing ball among some red and yellow trees that made the scene like something in a painting by Rousseau. It gave me quite a start seeing them; in the days just past we had forgotten the very existence of such things as poetry, music and children.

It was not right that children should see what we had seen in those days—and mercifully the majority of them had not done so. Kept safe at home or, whenever possible, sent out of the city for a few days, they would remember little of the disaster.

Our Gratitude

"Florence needs everybody's help, for Florence belongs to the whole world," said Richard Burton in Zeffirelli's documentary film. "However much we manage to do, it will be but little in return for all that dear city has given us. And everything we do will be done to hasten the return of that city which we all need so much..."

24

We have been deeply moved by all that the world has done and is still doing for our city. Thousands came to our aid, and thousands more sent help—governments and individuals, old Anglo-Saxons who wept for the Florence of years gone by, and younger folk who had spent some time here in their formative years and had here begun to grasp the meaning of the word "civilisation".

As La Pira said, a wonderful experiment was conducted in Florence during the emergency period. Young people, Italians and foreigners, fought together against the mud as they had probably never fought against prejudice or social injustice. For this time they were not inspired by some idealised abstraction, nor squabbling with a materialistic society that condemned them one minute and worshipped them the next; this time they were up against six hundred thousand tons of foul and all too tangible mud. They waded into it up to their eyebrows and toiled for long hours rescuing books, working with a wholehearted dedication that they had never brought to their studies, or their sports, or even their love affairs. They slept in couchettes in unheated trains on a siding at the station; they ate seldom and badly. But one of them saved a Velasquez; and many of them helped to save human lives, working in the hospitals and in the slums of the city.

Fahrenheit 451

The film "Fahrenheit 451" tells the story of our civilisation being threatened by a group of men who cause all books to be burnt in their determination to destroy completely the highest achievement of man's powers of expression. "We, too," wrote Pier Francesco Listri, "have witnessed a violent attempt to destroy things no less valuable than the material goods and possessions which are our chief preoccupation in these days... Now that material things are beginning once more to flow into the city, or are being laboriously extracted from the mud, it is time for something less tangible to be entered on the post-flood balance sheet:—that heritage which, over the centuries, has given Florence her character and her importance."

A few words should be said here before we go on to a list (albeit incomplete), of the damage caused to the city's cultural heritage by the flood.

During the worst days of the emergency many people, cultured and uncultured alike, were saying something like this: "It seems that money is available only for our works of art! When we've got twenty thousand people homeless, countless factories and workshops put out of action, families who have lost everything they possessed, don't come to me and talk about Cimabue! In this city we have works of art and to spare; the same cannot be said of houses..."

To this materialistic argument we may reply, no less materialistically, by saying that art and culture are without any doubt the city's greatest industry, her major provider of employment and her chief source of wealth. "Fifty thousand million lire a year," Ragghianti roared at an under secretary after the flood, "you just tell your minister that! Fifty thousand million a year in tourist revenue alone! We want to get out of this mess in a hurry, and by Heaven we will! We'll have all the museums open by Christmas, we'll have our exhibition of Italian art in February, and we'll hold the Maggio Musicale as planned in the Palazzo Strozzi—yes, in this pigsty!"

The Biblioteca Nazionale is not just a rather heavy-looking building full of books. Students and scholars come from all over the world for the sake of those books; they stay in Florence and provide work for the inhabitants of the city. The University is not a luxury; it is a source of wealth, both present and future. At the moment, of course, we are still wrestling with the immediate problems raised by the flood; the problems which will arise later have to be looked at from a different angle.

Florence is a living city, not merely a museum, and following a severe blow to the libraries, the University and the publishing houses (almost all of which suffered heavily), there could be a danger of young people leaving that city. "The damage done to the city's cultural and artistic heritage," wrote Adriano Seroni, "could lead to the violent disruption of a time-honoured pattern of life and activity. And since the activity in question could scarcely be carried on without the constant support of the region's industry and craftsmanship, it is evident that the productive efforts of centres all up and down the Arno are an integral part of the whole conception of Florence as a centre of art and civilisation..."

To conclude with the words of Giovanni Grazzini: "Together with the works of art, the libraries are the very life-blood of the city. Culture—in the shape of books, manuscripts, prints, drawings and journals—is the most vital factor in the life of Florence; it has given the city its raison d'être throughout history and is still the mainstay of the entire local economy, from the point of view of both industry and tourism."

Damage done to the City's Art treasures

Early estimates suggest that about 1,400 works of art were damaged. 850 of these were seriously affected and needed immediate attention: 221 paintings on wood, 413 paintings on canvas, 11 cycles of frescoes, 39 single frescoes, 31 frescoes removed from their original positions, 14 groups of sculpture, 122 individual sculptures, 22 sculptures in wood, and 22 illuminated codices.

These figures refer only to such works as are movable; so far it has been impossible to make any valid estimate with regard to buildings and structures.

The most seriously damaged works: Cimabue's "Crucifixion" in Santa Croce; frescoes by Paolo Uccello (Chiostro Verde, Santa Maria Novella), and Botticelli (Ognissanti Church); frescoes in the Cappellone degli Spagnoli, Pietro Lorenzetti, Simone Martini, Domenico Veneziano; Brunelleschi's model of the cupola in the Museo dell'Opera del Duomo. The Museo delle Scienze, the collection of musical instruments at the Museo Bardini, and the arms and armour of the Bargello were all seriously affected, as was also the Etruscan section of the Museo Archeologico. At the Baptistery several panels were detached from Andrea Pisano's door, and Ghiberti's Porta del Paradiso was damaged.

STATE ARCHIVES

The three hundred rooms and sixty kilometres of shelving contain the history of Florence and Tuscany from the days of the Communes up to the unification of Italy. About 10 % of the collection was damaged, but it is hoped that some 80 % of the damaged material may be restored. The most important documents affected include the archives of the suppressed monasteries, the archives of the Captain of the People from the fourteenth century onwards, the civic records of Tuscany from 1800 to 1860, and the police records from 1870 to 1900.

ARCHIVES OF THE OPERA DEL DUOMO

6,000 volumes of documents and 55 illuminated books of anthems submerged. About 80 % of the documents may be salvaged; 25 % of the anthem books are damaged beyond restoration.

LIBRARIES

Biblioteca Nazionale

About 1,300,000 items damaged—300,000 volumes and collections of journals, periodicals and miscellanies. The most important items buried in mud include the large volumes of the Palatina, the Magliabechi collection, which formed the nucleus of the Biblioteca Nazionale, all the collections of journals from the unification of Italy onwards (vital source material for modern historians), sixteenth century maps and atlases, and various catalogues.

Gabinetto Vieusseux

250,000 items, including all the letter-books of Vieusseux (first edition 1819), now quite irreplaceable. If no time is lost, as much as 50 % of the library may be salvaged.

Library of the Conservatorio di Musica Cherubini
Completely flooded; scores and libretti of seventeenth and eighteenth century lyric works seriously damaged.

Library of the Jewish Synagogue
14,000 seventeenth, eighteenth and nineteenth century volumes in urgent need of restoration, at an expected cost of 500 million lire. Serious damage was done to 90 of the 120 ancient rolls of parchment containing the entire Old Testament written by hand.

Library of the Accademia dei Georgofili
36,000 volumes damaged by water.

VALUABLE MANUSCRIPTS DESTROYED OR DAMAGED WHILE IN THE CITY FOR RESTORATION

Belonging to the civic library of Siena: a fourteenth century St Ambrose, a fifteenth century "De Veritate" of St Thomas, a fifteenth century Calderini.

Belonging to the Biblioteca Forteguerriana of Pistoia: the "Trattati Morali" of Albertano da Brescia translated by Soffredi Del Grazia; eighteen codices, including 2 Juvenal, 1 Priscian, 1 Pompeius Festus, 1 Cicero, 1 Valerius Maximus, 1 Boetius—some of these in the hand of the humanist Sozomeno.

THE UNIVERSITY

Nine of the 10 faculties suffered. Estimates of damage to scientific and teaching equipment as follows:

Arts: 260,000,000 lire. Half of the 100,000 books damaged by the flood.

Jurisprudence and Political Science: 250,000,000 lire. 30 % of the 8,300 volumes submerged were irreparably damaged.

Architecture: 60,000,000 lire. 60 % of the books damaged, many workrooms destroyed. Serious losses include collections of rare architectural reviews from 1910 to 1940.

Mathematical, Physical and Natural Sciences: 400,000,000 lire. Almost all the general and inorganic chemistry apparatus destroyed; that of organic chemistry completely destroyed.

Economics and Commerce: 20,000,000 lire. The Rosselli collection and the complete library of student theses submerged. 10 % of the books recoverable.

Medicine: 150,000,000 lire. The San Salvi clinic for nervous diseases, destroyed; severe damage to the skin and venereal disease clinic in the Via Alfani and the Institute of Phototherapy and Radiotherapy in the Via della Pergola.

Agriculture: 100,000,000 lire. Livestock completely lost; much apparatus destroyed. Damage to the library, and to the zootechnics, agriculture and microbiology laboratories.

Chemistry: Organic chemistry equipment and books badly damaged. 90 % of physical chemistry equipment destroyed, including many pieces of apparatus constructed in the institute, and consequently impossible to purchase. 90 % of the analytical chemistry equipment destroyed, together with 360 volumes, fortunately not rare, and half of all completed analyses.

Academy of Fine Arts: 10,000,000 lire for the damage to teaching material. 60 % of ancient manuscripts damaged by water, together with 3,000 ancient books.

The Months to Come
On the surface Florence will be much as she has always been, elegant and civilised. She will have her fashion shows, her art exhibitions, her Maggio Musicale. By spring ninety per cent of the hotels will be in perfect order; all the cinemas and many of the restaurants have already reopened. But, as President Torricelli of the Azienda di Turismo pointed out, the fact that there are lights in the shop windows does not in itself mean that the economy has returned to

full health. Florence and Tuscany, having few large industries but a great variety of small and medium-sized firms, had been slow to feel the effects of the nation's economic ills—and equally slow to recover from the aftermath of those ills. But factories were working on long-term commitments, the warehouses were full, craftsmen were working all out in anticipation of the summer to come, and it looked as if the chronic shortage of finance was being overcome.

Just as it was getting under way, the economic revival was hit by the flood, and it is difficult to tell at this stage how far the generous flow of loans, compensation and financial help will go towards getting things moving again. Certainly we have got off to a good start. Any craftsman who could afford to re-equip himself had only to clear the mud out of his workshop and start work again. According to Giovanni Bellini, national President of the Antique-dealers Association, the antique-dealers and furniture restorers have every reason to face the future with confidence—notwithstanding the fact that they are reputed to have suffered losses amounting to 2,000 million lire. A restorer would spend about 200,000 lire replacing lost equipment; there would be no lack of work for him. The antique-dealers, belonging as they do to an international market, have good hopes for recovery following the biennial exhibition of antiques to be held in September 1967.

The situation with regard to industry is rather more serious. The flood damage was particularly bad in the nearby industrial hinterland (where some five hundred firms suffered—certain of them to the extent of 500 million lire), and all down the Valdarno as far as Pisa. By contrast, the area along the Rifredi-Prato line was almost untouched. Nevertheless, credit has been made available, and production is restarting almost everywhere. The case of the publishing houses is typical. Almost all of them were seriously affected, but Universitaria Barbera, Le Monnier and Sansoni, to name but three, are already bringing out new titles, albeit in makeshift conditions. Florence's newspaper *La Nazione*, whose new plant suffered more than 500 million lire worth of damage, is once more appearing, thanks to technical and financial efforts which have been praised by the press of the entire nation.

Finally there is the question of public works. 30,000 million lire—the sum which has apparently been allocated for this task—is by no means excessive. Florence has shown considerable restraint in her demands—but she would not be so restrained if it appeared that these 30,000 million, or such other sums as have been subscribed and collected, were not being put to the best possible use. "The people of Florence," wrote Montanelli, "are unanimous that they themselves must decide how this money shall be spent. And this determination is inspired not so much by lack of confidence in the state, as by civic pride and the knowledge that they have a long and well-tried tradition of self-government behind them. The houses of Medici and Lorraine enjoyed relatively quiet lives partly because they never contested the right of the people of Florence to plan and build for themselves their streets and squares and bridges. And it seems to me that their obstinacy was justified by the results they achieved... Florence has her projects for the future and she wants to make this the occasion for carrying them out. Never before have I known her people so eager and self-confident as they are at this prospect of their city being restored, not by the state, but by themselves..."

But perhaps we should add one word more: let Florence by all means restore those elements of her past that were good and worthy—but let her also correct those errors and shortcomings which have hitherto been openly discussed only at occasional public meetings and in election campaigns. The flood uncovered many such shortcomings, and they must not be forgotten—even if we are at the moment only too anxious to forget what has happened by plunging back into the satisfactions of one of the most advanced consumer societies in the world. We must not forget the decaying houses of Gavinana, the squatters of Sorgane, the flooded countryside. The future of Florence depends upon our remembering.

What are the facts behind the flood?

A Computer could save Florence

If a few million lire had been wisely spent in the years preceding the flood, thousands of millions of lire worth of property, and perhaps even some human lives, could have been saved. It would cost very little to install apparatus capable of giving timely warning of events likely to lead to a disastrous flood such as that which burst upon Florence at dawn on November 4th.

Florence could not have defended herself, but she could have been warned. She could have been warned—and not at the last moment, when it was already too late, but several hours, perhaps even a whole day, in advance. And the warning could have been based not on mere human judgement, which is always open to controversy (as was that of the authorities involved on the night in question), but on calculations worked out by a computer. Nor would the type of computer required be unduly expensive.

"I see no reason," said Professor Livio Zoli, holder of Italy's only chair of forest hydrology, "why the readings of the thirteen hydrometers and the pluviometers situated up and down the Arno basin should not be concentrated in one room, so that we might have at all times a full knowledge of the various factors which would give warning of an approaching flood. One qualified man would be able to coordinate and interpret the data, possibly with the help of a computer.

"It is regrettable that in these modern times ninety per cent of the pluviometers installed in the Arno basin—incidentally, we have less than half the number we really need—should be of old-fashioned design and incapable of giving us all the information we require. Only ten per cent of them are self-registering."

What does a self-registering pluviometer cost? "Just over one hundred thousand lire."

What is the annual budget of the Professor's university department? "About two million lire."

What would it cost to set up the computer and the necessary pluviometers? "Fifty million lire at the most."

Just about what you would have to pay for a passably good footballer! Certainly less than it costs the city to make up a suburban road. And if those fifty million lire had been spent on scientific apparatus, thousands of millions of lire could have been saved.

The State

As these few details suggest, the flood waters not only devastated the city of Florence; they also laid bare the shortcomings of the state.

"Money is short," wrote Nicola Adelfi, "and there are innumerable things which urgently need doing—each more costly than the next. And this is why large areas of Italy are annually devastated by floods—for our governments, when faced with diverse needs, have never failed to shelve those problems which seemed to threaten us with no immediate danger... On the one hand we have a society which is mentally anticipating the future with all the impatience of a man who has just realised that his present home is poky and unhealthy and is determined to move into a modern and comfortable apartment—and on the other we have a national economy which is creaking and archaic."

But are we really so poor? Or do the events of November 1966 suggest that the various state bodies concerned—ministers, councillors, civil engineering authorities, and so on—have been incompetent in their handling of the resources, generous or otherwise, at their disposal? In other words, has the state made the best possible use of the finance provided by the nation's tax-payers?

Vittorio Gorresio, a political commentator who is by no means an opponent of the present government, replies to these questions as follows: "The organs of the state are charged, not so much with dishonesty, as with incompetence... To refer only to more recent measures, funds were allocated for the prevention of natural disasters in 1952 in a so-called river regulation plan, which came within the framework of a programme for agriculture and forestry. An original allocation of 1,454 thousand million lire was made, to be spent over thirty years, and this sum was advanced last year to 2,200 thousand million. Whether or not this amount was sufficient, it could be said that a notable and thoroughly worthy effort had been made. Nevertheless, a communication from Minister Mancini to the public works council makes it clear that in the programme's first ten years of operation only 289 thousand million were spent—little more than a third of what was available."

Penny wise and pound foolish, perhaps. We never cease boasting of our autostrade; sociologists are solemnly expressing their anxiety at our exuberant entry into the age of superfluous consumption—and meanwhile we have made no organic study of the country's geological condition. We are leaving our woodlands to their fate—but troops of schoolchildren annually celebrate a national tree festival with country walks and special essays in class. And our river embankments remain just as they were when they were constructed by the grand dukes, the doges and the popes.

We may console ourselves, however, with the thought that we have seriously entered the space race with our San Marco satellite.

Powerless for two days

The critical spirit of which so many Italians are possessed sometimes gives rise to a feeling that what the country needs is to have a "strong man" in control, capable of putting things to rights. There is even some grain of truth in the saying that Mussolini won power and popularity by making the trains run on time. This never entirely suppressed yearning for a "strong man" is merely another aspect of an age-old lack of confidence in the state, and in the days following the flood, when their city lay helpless beneath the mud and water, isolated and hungry, and the troops who were available could not act for lack of equipment, even the people of Florence felt the need for some mythical general to take charge of things, notwithstanding their traditional love of liberty and intolerance of authority.

Commune, prefecture and army all aspired to take command of operations—but none of them had full power, let alone the means that would have enabled them to be effective. The first ones to have a coherent plan for relief work, the clearing of débris and measures to be taken against the threat of an epidemic, were in fact the military authorities—and then only for the city's hinterland, where injured,

30

starving, half-frozen people were still in danger as much as eighty hours after the flood had reached its climax. At San Donnino, San Mauro and Brozzi the army took full responsibility and successfully carried out their missions.

Meanwhile, as the newspaper *L'Espresso* pointed out, the government was concerning itself with the events of Armed Forces Day: parades, religious ceremonies, colours being trooped, unknown warriors being honoured, minutes of silence being scrupulously observed. President of the Council, Vice-president, ministers and secretaries were all participating in these rites. And when the few telephones still functioning in the flooded areas were connected with the government offices in Rome, those offices were empty; and when in desperation the home telephone numbers of the officials concerned were tried, the result was much the same.

Here is what Mattei wrote for the edition of *La Nazione* which appeared, having been printed in Bologna, on Sunday, November 6th: "The day before yesterday Finance Minister Pieraccini and Under-Secretary of the Interior Ceccherini (the former a Florentine, the latter a Pisan now living in Friuli), boldly faced the dangers and uncertainties of an eventful journey and drove through a veritable downpour to reach the isolated city of Florence. At the Comiliter H.Q. they held a conference with General Centofanti, military commander of the Tuscany-Emilia area. After this they mounted the turret of a tank and by way of the Via Camillo Cavour, which was a raging torrent of water, reached the Prefecture, where another conference was held. Somehow they managed to get through on the telephone to ministers in Rome and military commanders in other parts of Italy, and dramatic conversations took place. Anyone who was present at those conferences and heard those telephone conversations can testify to the urgent and wholehearted efforts which these few men made to pierce the thick skin of the state and force it to disgorge means of succour which it either lacks, or at least never has available at times of emergency.

"Their efforts were impassioned, admirable, exemplary; but they met with incredible difficulties. The control-room was there all right, and the controls were operated by eager and capable hands—but behind them there lay a great deal of insensibility and inefficiency. As late as yesterday morning, Saturday, in the flooded areas across the Arno, entire families were still appealing for bread and water; and all they saw was an occasional passing boatload of photographers. It was not until the following afternoon that supply and relief work began to be decently organised.

"How many millions of words have we used discussing civil defence projects! And yet no country could be worse protected against natural catastrophes. The experience of Florence is eloquent enough. At a certain hour on a certain day a swollen river overflows into a great city... No one has seen the river rise. No one has estimated the danger. No one has given the alarm. And yet rivers do not overflow at a moment's notice; their level rises gradually. And when the water reaches a dangerous level, it ought not to be too difficult to warn the people likely to be affected... Why was this not done in Florence?"

Why no Warning? Unshaven, muddy, with glazed and staring eyes, the people of Florence asked themselves this question when they went to buy their newspapers that Sunday morning. The sun was shining, and the first stenches were beginning to rise from the mud. The papers were being sold from piles heaped up on the steps of buildings; scores of kiosks had been smashed and swept away by the flood.

As the days went by and people began to be aware of the deeper and less obvious wounds inflicted on the city, more and more voices took up the question. There was anger, then rage, in some of the worst hit areas of the city, and it was only the announcement that the magistrature had ordered an inquiry into this point and into the matter of the dams that momentarily checked the spreading unrest.

31

Perhaps it would be as well here to let the people involved in this "non-warning" speak for themselves. I have had many opportunities of collecting their evidence at both first and second hand.

When I spoke to Mayor Bargellini we were behind the Palazzo Vecchio. He raised one hand and indicated a street name-plate. We were in one of the streets in the quarter in which Vasco Pratolini set his novel *Cronache di poveri amanti*: the Via dei Leoni. "Look at that!" said the Mayor. "That name-plate is fixed to the wall four metres above the ground—and it is black with oil! The flood water was higher than that! We were all going around that night of November 3rd to 4th. We watched the river rise and saw the water beginning to get through the parapets. Then, when we were stuck in the Palazzo Vecchio, we watched the water till it was about a metre deep. Every single one of us, from boyhood onwards, had had experience of floods; and always, at a certain point, the water had begun to subside. We naturally thought the same thing was going to happen this time."

But would it have been technically possible to warn the city?

"Someone suggested ringing the Martinella bell. Ridiculous! People would have taken it for part of the November 4th celebrations. Loudspeaker vans? At eight o'clock in the morning we did not think we would be justified in raising a general alarm; we might easily have caused an unnecessary panic. By ten o'clock, when it was clear that what was happening was worse than anything in living memory (worse, indeed, than anything we could have imagined), the people were all too well aware of the situation! In any case the roads were impassable by that time. Through the centre of the city, and elsewhere, torrents of oily, muddy water were tearing along at sixty kilometres an hour, carrying all before them."

In the early hours of November 4th the Prefect and the Chief of Police also had a discussion on the advisability or otherwise of raising the alarm. But, as it later became known, the idea was soon dismissed. In the first place the danger did not seem to justify such a course of action; and secondly—even apart from the difficulty of rousing a city of half a million people in a limited amount of time—it was thought that hundreds of lives might well be lost in a sudden mad rush of cars making for the hills and the autostrada.

The policy which was followed, then, was the one which at the time seemed most sensible to the authorities.

No one realised

If Florence had died for ever beneath the suffocating mud, these words could have stood as her epitaph.

But they will not stand up as an explanation for what happened. The edition of *La Nazione* which went on the streets at seven o'clock on the morning of November 4th (and which few people had the opportunity of buying and reading), bore the dramatic headline: "The Arno overflows at Florence" and went on: "The city is in danger of being flooded. At 5.30 this morning water streamed over the embankments, flooding the Via dei Bardi, the Borgo San Jacopo, the Volta dei Tintori and the Corso dei Tintori, the Lungarno delle Grazie and the Lungarno Acciaiuoli. Many families are evacuating their homes. The river-banks at Rovezzano and Compiobbi were overtopped shortly after 1 a.m. The Via Villamagna and the aqueduct plant at Anconella were invaded a short time later, and certain areas of the city are in danger of losing their water supply. There are indications that the day ahead may bring drama unparalleled in the history of the city. At 4.30 a.m. military units were ordered to stand by to cope with a possible emergency situation."

By 6 a.m. the emergency was an established fact. The carabinieri, for example, had no further boats at their disposal and were appealing to private citizens for more. Fire-engines were trapped at Sieci, Compiobbi and all the other points to which they had hastened in their efforts to save life. The technicians of the civil engineering department had already established that the level of the Arno had risen by six metres between 9 p.m. on the 3rd and 3 a.m. on the 4th. A hundred men of the mobile police had left for Incisa, where terrified people were already climbing onto their roofs for safety.

The authorities, then, were all at action stations—the Prefect, the Chief of Police, the civil engineering department, the General. Not one of them was absent through not having been informed, or through any reluctance to do his duty. But not one of them realised in time what was happening.

Why the Goldsmiths?

Nevertheless, some people were warned that night and were able to make some attempt to save their property from the flood. These were the jewellers and goldsmiths of the Ponte Vecchio. And in the days to come they were the object of at least part of the resentment felt by the thousands who had not been warned and who had in consequence lost homes, shops, furniture, motorcars, and in some cases even been bereaved. Only a few of the goldsmiths managed to reach their shops in time to save the choicest articles in their stock, and many of them have seen a thriving family business reduced to a shattered ruin through which they can now look down upon the sullen and indifferent river passing below. But the fact remains that somebody warned them of the danger.

One of those who gave warning was Romildo Cesaroni, an elderly night watchman who, as he hails from Longarone, seems fated to be involved in natural calamities. Every night, regardless of the weather, he cycles round his beat, tucking slips of paper into doorways as evidence of his having checked the premises. One of his particular duties is that of warning the Ponte Vecchio jewellers if ever the river begins to look dangerous. He knows them all personally by this time; he knows which of them will come running at the first hint of danger, and which of them will reply: "Thanks, Cesaroni, but not to worry! We'll have a drink together in the morning..."

The Arno was a fearful spectacle that night, and Cesaroni had no doubts at all. He began telephoning: "I've never seen the river like this before; it will have the bridge down this time."

Here is the dramatic story of the Piccini family, who have been jewellers for generations, as told by Signora Albertina Piccini-Risaliti:

"We were still awake just before 1 a.m. when the night watchman telephoned. 'You'd better come, Signora,' he said; 'the Arno looks terribly dangerous.' We grabbed five or six suitcases and tore off in the car. It was a dangerous ride, for there were plenty of other cars speeding about. It was pouring when we got to the bridge. The watchman was standing at one corner, and there were several little Fiats parked close by with their headlights blazing. About fifteen rough-looking young men got out of them and started prancing about behind us, laughing and shouting abuse. 'Just in the nick of time! The bridge'll be down in ten minutes. Why don't you give us some of those lovely jewels? Look at 'em running!' I was frightened, and I called to my husband, but he was already at the door of the shop. He could not get it open; perhaps it was excitement, but the lock seemed to be stuck and it took him several minutes to turn the key. It must have been just on two when we entered the shop. The floor was shaking terribly under our feet, and outside I could see tree-trunks charging along and looking as if they were going to crash in through the window. Our first inclination was to run away. We could hear awful thuds and bangs going on, and the floor was shaking and shaking. The water could not have been more than a metre below us. We spent ten minutes or so in the first room, grabbing the first things that came to hand and articles belonging to our clients. When I think now of all the things we left behind, all the things we lost, I could weep. My husband shut himself in the office, telling me to go and take the cases safe home. And I kept shouting to him to come too. Then two carabinieri came, and they banged at the door, too. 'Come away! The bridge is in danger!' The boys were still outside, and a friend saw me home. I picked up some more suitcases and went back to the bridge, getting there about half past three. The lights had gone out, and it was pitch dark and pouring with rain. But there were a lot of cars with their headlights on. Some of the cars belonged to other jewellers, friends of ours—but I don't know about the others. We collected up some more things, but then the bridge started shaking so violently that we thought it was going to collapse at any moment, and we ran for it. The last thing I remember is a huge tree-trunk and a Fiat 1100 butting at the window of the shop; I thought for a moment I had gone mad. Some people were still on the bridge, and the carabinieri were shouting: 'At your own risk and peril!' And we shouted at the carabinieri: 'Why don't you go and warn other people? Why don't you get in your cars and go and give the alarm?' And they replied—and you could see they were embarrassed—'We have no orders.' So we ran and started telephoning those friends of ours who still knew nothing of what was happening. Some of them were in bed and answered sleepily—'Oh, it's nothing serious. You always did worry too much!' Some of them did not even answer the phone; perhaps they had gone shooting, or off to Sanremo for the weekend...''

Two or three details stand out from the events of that night: the carabiniere who said, "We have no orders"—when the flood was rising and the bridge was trembling beneath the onslaught of the waters; the official of the civil engineering department who, as early as two o'clock, found the situation "worrying"; those people who were either incredulous or ludicrously optimistic when the news reached them by telephone. These three examples are typical of people's reactions to the drama that was gathering about their city.

In this twentieth century of atomic power and moon rockets, Florence is the only great European city to have been invaded and laid waste by a flood. And no one had orders to give the alarm. These words, too, might have served as an epitaph.

The Heavens opened Special correspondents of Italian and foreign newspapers were all agreed that never in their lives had they heard such tremendous and colourful swearing as they heard in Florence in the two or three days following the flood.

But my favourite memory is of a little old man I met in the market place of Sant'Ambrogio on the morning of November 5th. The water had gone down during the night, and ruined cars and lorries and wrecked house-fronts were beginning to emerge from the mud. All who could were wading through the mess in search of their possessions. The old man could find no trace of the battered and aged van he had used for transporting vegetables. He clenched his fists and raised them to heaven; tears started from his eyes and in a broken, scarcely audible voice he exclaimed: "Words fail me!"

The elements had really excelled themselves this time—even though it must be admitted that human errors and omissions had also been a contributory factor. If we try to analyse the combination of circumstances that led to the disaster, we soon find that a remarkable series of meteorological phenomena were involved.

In less than twenty-four hours—from 1.40 p.m. on November 3rd to 1 p.m. on the 4th—more than 190 mm. (about 7 ½ inches) of rainwater fell on the city. This was higher than any figure ever registered in Florence, and the downpour was certainly one of the major factors contributing to the flood. To give some idea of the quantity of water involved, it will be enough to mention that the average annual rainfall in Florence, based on statistics kept from 1813 to 1964, is 823 mm. (about 33 inches), which means that almost a quarter of a year's rain fell in the space of one day. The previous record for a day's rainfall in Florence was 100 mm. (about 4 inches). The flood of November 1966 was accompanied by almost twice that amount.

But equally important, according to the experts, was the fact that rain of equal or even greater intensity fell throughout the region traversed by the Arno and its tributaries.

The Long Rain, a story by that master of science fiction Ray Bradbury, begins as follows: "The rain continued. It was a hard rain, a perpetual rain, a sweating and steaming rain; it was a mizzle, a downpour, a fountain, a whipping at the eyes, an undertow at the ankles; it was a rain to drown all rains and the memory of rains. It came by the pound and the ton, it hacked at the jungle and cut the trees like scissors and shaved the grass and tunnelled the soil and molted the bushes. It shrank men's hands into the hands of wrinkled apes; it rained a solid glassy rain, and it never stopped."

But the rain in Florence was not science fiction; and it fell, not on the planet Venus, but on one of the richest areas of this world's civilisation—on churches and museums and carefully tended fields and men who had inherited the works and spirit of the Renaissance.

Rain was not the only phenomenon to make an impression that night of November 3rd-4th. There were others, too—some scientifically registered, some to be found only in the anguished accounts of individuals.

We visited the Ximeniano observatory, and the director Father Mazzantini, with his cassock hitched up over his mud-caked boots, spoke to us. "At the climax of the flood there was a strange concurrence of meteorological phenomena. At midnight on November 2nd the barometer was realing 760 (about 30.40 inches). It then began to fall steadily until it reached 740·5 (about 29.60 inches) at 11 a.m. on the 4th, after which it started to rise. The temperature also behaved peculiarly. From 12-13° C it suddenly shot up at 11 a.m. on that same day to 17° C, whereupon it subsided gradually to more normal levels. The reason for all this was a cyclone which crossed the Tyrrhenian Sea on the night of the 2nd and was followed over Tuscany by a huge mass of warm and humid air." The director concluded that, meteorologically speaking, the disaster had been quite unpredictable.

A workman of the engineering department who had been at San Donnino from 6 p.m. on November 3rd gave his impressions as follows: "During the night we were working to strengthen the banks. All at once a terrific wind got up and tore at us like a whirlwind. There was thunder and lightning circling around us, too. The engineer said he thought it must be a tornado. I've never seen anything like it. It was about an hour after that that the flood wave reached us; the Macinante overflowed, and I just don't know how we managed to escape."

In Florence itself there were tales of roars and rumblings coming from the bowels of the earth.

The flood of November 4, 1966 beat all records, except possibly that for loss of life. And there have been plenty of floods in Florence. In various parts of the historic city centre there are tablets set into walls commemorating the height reached by the waters, and we can get a vivid idea of the most recent flood by comparing it with these records of the past:

Junction of Via delle Casine and Via Ghibellina—3.11.1844: 1·84 m. 4.11.1966: 4·95 m.

Junction of Via San Remigio and Via dei Neri—4.11.1333: 4·22 m. 4.11.1966: 4·92 m.

Junction of Piazza Santa Croce and Via Verdi—13.9.1557: 3·50 m. 4.11.1966: 4·45 m.

Via di Villamagna, in the outskirts of the city, also follows this pattern—3.11.1844: 1·53 m. 4.11.1966: 4·17 m.

I put this question to a variety of people in positions of responsibility.

The Mayor flung his arms wide and said: "It would be the same story over again. Exactly the same. And you only have to look at the map to see why. The Arno runs through hills, and the bed of the river is like a sort of gutter.

Suppose it happened again?

35

If the water fills this gutter, it overflows, and Florence is devastated—just as it was on November 4th. The city has no possible defence against a flood of such proportions. Believe me, it is not a question of human improvidence. If we were prepared to spend the money, technology might be able to do something to defend the Po Valley, but not our city."

Florence is subject to floods. She lives under the constant threat of the Arno. And, even today, statistics are all we have to defend her with. Instead of sound riverbanks, dikes and flood relief-channels, we have statistics. They assure us that we can relax for a century or so; there is not much chance of us getting a really bad flood, like this one, till about 2060. There might be a medium-sized one around 1990—a dozen deaths, perhaps, and a hundred thousand million lire worth of damage—but nothing to cause any alarm.

Is everything to remain, then, as it was before? It cannot be denied that many people in Florence today are watching events with irony and suspicion. This may be a result of the state's poor showing during the emergency, or it may be an example of the Florentines' tendency to debunk the authorities and their traditional reluctance to dwell gloomily on the past. The fact remains that a good many people, for one reason or another, completely agree with Mayor Bargellini.

Technical experts have slightly different ideas. "The engineering department," explained Lensi Orlandi, the Commune's chief engineer, with a smile, "is responsible for construction works on the rivers—banks, bridges, and so on—and they base their decisions on the highest flood level recorded in the past ten years. If they follow the same rule now, they will have to replace the embankment parapets with ramparts four metres high."

On one thing we are all agreed: the city has paid too dearly for the errors and omissions of the past.

Professor Livio Zoli, who holds the country's only chair of forest hydrology, received me at the Faculty of Agriculture one Sunday morning.

I asked if there was anything that could be done to avert possible future disasters.

"We must first have a few words of explanation," said the Professor. "Hydraulic works are very often not designed to cope with the maximum potential danger. In the Po Valley, for example, it is considered preferable to accept the damage rather than spend the vast sums that would be required to take effective measures against flooding. No such calculation can be made in the case of Florence. If it were only a question of houses, land and factories, a purely economic criterion might be justifiable; but here we are dealing with treasures that are unique and irreplaceable. We have no choice. At all costs we must ensure safety in the years to come. And we must take the flood of November 4, 1966 as the basis of our calculations—not the lesser inundations of the past. The problems involved are fantastic, and the solutions proposed may sound like science fiction—but they are technically possible.

"1) *Scrapping the weirs.*

"As far back as the Middle Ages, writers were pointing out the danger of these weirs. The two which remain in the Florence of today, moreover, serve no useful function. They provide no motive power for mills and are not used for fulling. Getting rid of them would mean remaking the foundations of all the bridges and reconstructing the river embankments. This would be no light matter—but it would be preferable to lining the river with ramparts four metres high!

"2) *Creation of reservoirs.*

"Reservoirs must be constructed along the course of the river. But it is important to realise that these reservoirs must have an exclusively defensive function and must not be expected to produce electric power like those of Levane and La Penna. The two functions, indeed, are diametrically opposed to each other. If the reservoirs are to be valid defences, they must be empty at the onset of winter; whereas to obtain power they must be full. The E.N.E.L. may be a nationalised concern, but its prime function is to produce electricity. The state should construct at least ten purely defensive reservoirs. I do not deny that it would be a costly business, nor that it would be hard to find suitable sites—but it must be done.

"3) *Safe outlets.*

"Almost five hundred years ago Leonardo da Vinci was working on this subject. And in those days the river had at least some room to expand; today it is tightly hemmed in by both hills and built-up areas. During the flood, of course, the Arno found its own outlet! It overflowed first on the right, at Rovezzano; all the water that came over the Lungarno Acciaioli and the Lungarno Archibusieri swept through the city; the Mugnone blocked it off, and it returned to the Arno up by the Cascine. The only possibility nowadays, as I see it, would be to construct a huge underground tunnel capable of draining off at least 1,000 cubic metres per second."

The Neglect of the Forests Giustino Fortunato once wrote that "a nation that does not believe in God does not plant trees." And he added: " Let us return to the old days... Let us renew our old traditions of stock-raising, re-establish our pasturelands, our woods and coppices—those dense forests which, two centuries ago, extended from one side of Lucania to the other, and which we have thoughtlessly stripped from the unstable slopes of our mountains."

Lucio Susmel, Professor of Forestry at the University of Padua, writes as follows: "Our forests and woodlands are at present in poor condition and are by no means in keeping with the morphology and erratic rainfall of the peninsula. This is why, notwithstanding the fact that we have no less than five and a half million hectares of woodland, our country is both short of timber and ill-protected against flooding. If it is not too seriously interfered with, the floor of a forest acts as a giant sponge, from which any water not used by the trees is able to trickle a little at a time... But if the woodlands are weakened by excessive felling or by over-intensive grazing, an unfortunate combination of weather conditions can lead to an extensive, but not necessarily extraordinary, rainfall immediately pouring vast masses of water into the principal river basins. And though we still have no exact data for the recent downpour, there are indications that, as on previous occasions, the events followed this pattern."

Professor Guglielmo Benfratello of the University of Palermo wrote as follows in the *Corriere della Sera*: "Though deforestation certainly contributed to the unbalance of the river basins and generally aggravated the situation, not even a magical renewal of the forests could have noticeably diminished the floods of the past few days or lessened the gravity of their effects... We must conclude that, in addition to the long-term measures to be taken, vigorous and well-coordinated methods of procedure should be prepared for use in time of emergency. Coordinated gauging systems, frequent exchanges of information between weather stations and control-points along watercourses and at artificial lakes, cooperation at all levels between the ministries of public works, defence and the interior—if such tactics were adopted, natural hazards could be foreseen and technical staffs could be alerted in good time. Reasonable and valid decisions could then be taken about such matters as the opening of hydroelectric dams—actions whose effects it is impossible to calculate when one only has information about conditions in the immediate vicinity..."

All this is precisely what was lacking at the time of our flood.

Professor Zanini also wrote in the *Corriere della Sera*: "What we need is an overall plan for catchment basins which will take in the whole range of hydraulic problems, including that of the utilisation of water, industrial, agricultural and domestic... Nor should we forget the fact that a large number of different authorities may today be operating within a single district—land-improvement authorities, provincial reforestation councils, the national forestry board, various public undertakings, development corporations, and so on, as well as the communes and councils of towns and villages both in the valleys and in the mountains. To avoid confusion, clashes and the dissipation of effort in carrying out both public and private works, it is to be hoped that these many authorities will be condensed into a smaller number prepared to collaborate closely with one another. Such a move would be in the interests of the entire nation."

So many voices, so many recommendations! And at the time of the tragedy there was only silence and impotence.

Inquiry and Responsibility

When this volume appears a grave question will still remain to be answered. The inquiry ordered by the Florence magistrature has grown and grown—just as the waters of the Arno grew during the first few days of November. The scope of the inquiry has been steadily widened, as more and more issues have been raised, and it now extends to problems, individuals, localities and periods which at first seemed quite remote from the matter in hand, but which are in fact intimately connected with it. Among past events to be examined will be the beginnings of the hydroelectric dams at La Penna and Levane, and the use made of them by the private company Selt Valdarno and, following the nationalisation of electricity (at a cost of about one and a half billion lire, which could undoubtedly have been better spent), the E.N.E.L.

It will probably also be necessary for the inquiry to expand geographically, with similar commissions set up at Pisa, Arezzo and Grosseto. Hundreds of people have already been interviewed, and much of the evidence—even some of the most important evidence—has been contradictory. This is not to say that witnesses have been dishonest. Anyone in the Valdarno that tragic night experienced a shock which will not easily be forgotten, a shock which may have banished customary restraints and confused people's sense of time and sequence. After such experiences it is difficult for witnesses to remain completely unaffected by rumours, public opinion, ancient fears and newly grown resentments.

It is the inquiry's task to establish the truth—and in many cases the data they have to go on are inadequate. It is known, for example, that the automatic measuring equipment (which in any case existed at only one of the two reservoirs), was not working and that entries were made in the registers by hand. If both basins had been equipped with modern measuring apparatus, the relevant information could now be obtained with speed and accuracy.

It was in the hope of being able to operate with speed and accuracy that the Public Prosecutor, Doctor Nicola Serra, looked forward to an early conclusion of the inquiry. He was sadly disillusioned at finding so many vaguenesses and inconsistencies in his material, and the inquiry will now clearly be a lengthy business, bent on "getting to the botton of things".

Will the inquiry conclude by naming "guilty men" who, after the months of investigation, will be brought to justice in response to public demand? Will it uncover facts which will lead to civil or criminal charges being brought against certain individuals?

Our personal opinion is that it will not. And one scarcely knows whether to applaud or bemoan the fact. Certainly our peace of mind would be destroyed if it were proved that we had been in the hands of individuals whose irresponsibility had led to a disaster of such magnitude.

But if, as seems probable, no individuals are named as having been responsible, it does not mean that we can shrug our shoulders and talk about "fate" or the "wrath of God" and accept the view that the whole thing was completely unpredictable. It does mean that we must face up to the fact that there existed a whole series of errors, omissions and shortages—for which the state must ultimately be held responsible.

Certain things seem to be emerging from the inquiry: the inadequacy and obsolescence of measuring equipment and communications (*La Stampa* claimed that a single telephone could have prevented disaster at Grosseto); the slow progress in the construction of defence works (ten thousand million lire spent on the Arno at Pisa, building a relief outlet channel which was left unfinished for lack of a mere two hundred million); the ambiguous nature of the reservoirs (expected to produce electricity and at the same time act as a defence—when it is widely recognised that the two functions are incompatible); uncertainty as to who should have power to take decisions in a crisis (the E.N.E.L. or the civil engineering department in the case of the dams, for example).

One cannot help reflecting that the same things are suggested by matters which have been touched upon in these pages: those two days after the flood when there was no proper relief organisation; the thousands of millions of lire allocated to the river regulation plan and only partly used; the multiplicity of authorities more or less responsible for our forests; the ludicrously insufficient funds made available for research in the field of forest hydrology.

All too often, in Italy, plans and projects of fundamental importance get discussed—and then shelved until it is too late. We seem to devote our entire energies to one nine-days wonder after another. It may be Longarone, it may be Fiumicino, it may be the Alto Adige—it may be a flood. We throw ourselves into the matter with zeal and generosity and a sincere desire to put things right. But always we are after the event; always energy and finances are dissipated. More and more people are losing confidence in the authorities and adopting an attitude of ironical detachment. And in the meantime scandals and disasters show no sign of decreasing in number.

The Dams

The Levane dam stands solitary at the end of a gorge. It is, in itself, neither beautiful nor terrifying. You approach it along a narrow road marked with a sign that says "No Entry". All around, ironically enough, there is a healthy and well-tended reafforestation area. When I went up there two days after the flood, it certainly did not strike me as a "Kafkaesque structure", as one English journalist described it, even though it was raining at the time and the whole place seemed deserted. The reservoir was half empty (very different from the night of the flood!), but even so the roaring of the water was tremendous when the sluice-gates slowly opened. A few hundred metres away as the crow flies there were motor-cars speeding down the Autostrada del Sole. Down river from the dam the banks of the Arno looked as if they had been blown up—a souvenir of November 4th. Trees had been uprooted, but a little shrine still stood tall and intact. The water had traced a greenish yellow line across the walls of the houses and the inn right up under the dam.

Some sort of official in a camel-hair overcoat stood beneath a huge black umbrella deferentially held by a silent subordinate. He was talking to Lorenzo Raffaelli.

Lorenzo Raffaelli is one of the principal witnesses. A clear-eyed, deep-voiced native of the Valdarno, he has spent more than sixty years in the company of the river. By now he had told his story many times—to the E.N.E.L., the police, the magistrature, journalists, relatives, friends, priest. When the mysterious officials left, it was our turn to ask him what had happened at the dam in the hours immediately preceding the flooding in Florence.

"They should have opened the dam at 2 p.m. on the Thursday," he said, "not 5 p.m. At 2 p.m. they could have unloaded some water, and that would have given them a better chance of coping with things later. By 5 p.m. there was already a terrifying quantity of water in there. It must have been about ten to five when I heard the siren—that's the warning signal for the opening of the sluice-gates. The water was pouring out all the rest of the afternoon."

In the *Sunday Times* David Leitch and Philip Knightley wrote as follows: "Its officials—(i.e. the officials at the Levane dam)—had realised at 7 p.m., two hours before the flooding decision was taken, that their generating equipment was in serious danger. The water level had already reached 167 metres—only half a metre below the officially prescribed danger-point." And they go on to quote Lorenzo Raffaelli's thirty-year-old daughter Ida: "The siren sounded again at nine, and I went out to look. I was appalled to see the gates slowly opening and immediately an enormous wall of water started coming down the Arno towards us. I screamed to my sister and we ran for our lives."

This account does not agree with the one her father gave to *L'Europeo*. Nor does it agree with what he told us: "I heard the siren for the second time about 11 p.m. and I realised then that something serious was going to happen. I sent the women away from the house. They begged me to go with them, but I refused to leave my home and my possessions. As they left we could hear the roaring of the water. I pulled down the shutters and closed the door. Then, behind the door, I stacked up the heaviest bits of furniture that I could manage to move and went upstairs. I wrapped myself in a blanket and sat at the window. The water was rising higher and higher. At last I left the window and went to lie down. But I didn't get a wink of sleep. Every so often I went to see how things were going, and I had the impression that the river reached its highest point sometime between 1 a.m. and 6 a.m. After that it began to go down, and by eight o'clock I was able to put on a pair of boots and venture out. The river bank was destroyed, and there were smashed tree-trunks all over the place. During the day people started coming up here with terrifying stories of what had happened in other places. Some said that the La Penna dam had collapsed, and others told us that dozens of people had been drowned at Incisa."

These two accounts are clearly contradictory; and perhaps the most serious complaint against them is that they do not agree about the time of the second alarm.

One point on which many witnesses do agree is that the Levane reservoir was particularly full in the days preceding the flood. Some people are even ready to explain why this was so; but their "explanations" (such as that the army were conducting bridging exercises over the river below the dam), are as yet quite unsubstantiated by any evidence. Others accept the fullness of the reservoir as perfectly normal in view of the E.N.E.L.'s function of producing electricity. Various engineers have stated that one reservoir cannot be expected to produce electricity and serve as a defence against flooding. Empty reservoir equals safety; full, or nearly full, reservoir equals electric power; it is as simple as that. The *Sunday Times* interviewed E.N.E.L. officials (who adopted a "fatalistic attitude" when pressed), and—though it is rather difficult to imagine any functionary saying such things—"the burthen of their replies was: 'It didn't matter that we opened the gates and kept them open. We could not have held the water back. It would have gone over the top. Anyway, we're not in charge of the river; our job is to produce electricity.'"

Can we perhaps work our way towards the truth, basing our reasoning, as the official inquiry must do, on the evidence and statements of individuals? The reservoirs at La Penna and Levane were full on the evening of the Thursday, and things seem to have come to a head between 6 p.m. and 8 p.m. *La Nazione* of November 7th put this time somewhat later in its reconstruction of the events: "The La Penna reservoir was completely full, and the sluice-gates were duly opened to drain off some of the excess water coming down from the rivers. The dam could not cope with a load of such proportions. They tried to raise the gates above the stipulated seven metres, but it was not possible owing to the tremendous pressure exerted by the water. The level rose higher and higher, until the water flowed over the rim of the dam. The structure stood up admirably to the strain, and mercifully the horror of another Longarone in the Valdarno was averted. But the water had to go somewhere, and inexorably it swept down from La Penna to the next barrier, the Levane dam. And the Levane dam in turn must inevitably have overflowed."

The *Sunday Times* was rather more dramatic in its assertions: "A special Sunday Times inquiry here this week has established that the Florence flood disaster was made worse by the release of water from a hydroelectric dam into the River Arno. This occurred just eight hours before the river first burst its banks in the city at 5 a.m. on Friday, November 4... At 9 p.m. the previous evening, the E.N.E.L. (Ente Nazionale Energia Elettrica), a nationalised authority hydroelectric plant at Levane, 35 miles up river from Florence, opened its gates because it could no longer hold back flood waters threatening to burst the dam, holding five million cubic yards of water. At this moment it became a certainty that the Arno in Florence was eventually going to flood, fed both by the newly released dam waters and the Arno's many swollen tributaries. Yet no advance warning was given to the city's inhabitants.

"One highly important point is that the State Civil Engineer from Arezzo, Dr Giovanni Maioli, was present in the Levane dam control room at the time when the gates were open. He would have been consulted about the effects this action would have on the Arno, as the river itself is the Civil Engineering Department's responsibility. There is no doubt that Dr Maioli was in contact with his civil engineering colleagues in Florence. They, in turn, advised the Prefect that some flooding was likely. Only the Prefect is empowered to issue a general alarm.

"This means that all the relevant civil authorities knew that the flood was going to hit Florence a clear eight hours before it did. Why was no emergency plan of any kind put into operation?"

It is impossible to calculate with any accuracy the influence which the water released by the dams may have had on the flooding of the city at dawn on November 4th.

When you ask their opinion, the people of the Valdarno shake their heads and say: "Even the authorities don't know how much water those reservoirs can hold. But they are devils, both of them. The best thing would be to get rid of them. We'd all be better off; we'd have to go back to candles—no electric power—but we wouldn't have the constant threat of being drowned."

This fear of the dams found expression at Figline Valdarno just before midday on Saturday, November 5th. A man—some say it was a policeman—rushed into the street shouting: "Telephone call from Levane. The dam has burst! Every man for himself!" The news spread in an instant, and hundreds of people began running for the hills. On one of these hills stands the old Serristori hospital. The director, Dr Renato Martini, takes up the story: "Though I knew there was nothing in the rumour, I ran to the hospital, thinking that people might well be hurt in the rush. A great crowd of frenzied people arrived. It was obvious that the whole thing was no more than a rumour—if the dam really had given way, the water would have arrived by this time. But a dozen or more women collapsed with hysterics..."

As soon as the first murmurings were heard about the opening of the dam gates, the E.N.E.L. put out an official statement which was, perhaps, just a little too detailed and dogmatic: "The quantity of water by which Florence was assailed in the twenty-four hours of November 4th can be reckoned at approximately 250 million cubic metres—120 million from the upper Arno, and the remainder from tributaries joining the main stream down river from the dams. It must be pointed out that, compared with this figure of 250 million cubic metres, the capacity of the two reservoirs—thirteen million cubic metres—is quite insignificant... It has also been ascertained that, during the flood period, the water level in the reservoirs was kept unchanged by regular and progressive operation of the normal outlet mechanism, and that it was not necessary to open the gates to their fullest extent..."

Other authorities claim that the volume of water which poured into Florence was 400 million cubic metres, and that the capacity of the reservoirs was some nine million cubic metres greater than that asserted by the E.N.E.L. And the technical investigations of engineer Masci of the public works department (quoted in *Vie Nuove*), indicated that between 2 a.m. and 4 a.m. of November 4th—that is to say at the most critical time—the outflow of the dams rose from 1,800 to 2,100 cubic metres per second. "In the extreme conditions then prevailing, and bearing in mind the swollen state of the Arno and its tributaries, it has been estimated by E.N.E.L. technicians that between 4,000 and 4,500 cubic metres of water per second were reaching Florence—a volume markedly in excess of what could reasonably be supported. The technicians at the dam warned the civil engineering department, and they in turn passed the warning on to the police and the prefecture."

And here once again the threads of the story become tangled. Was the warning couched in terms sufficiently urgent? Were the technicians anyway in a position to know what was happening all up and down the course of the river? Can it be said that there existed an efficient organisation for the collection and transmission of information—or that there was an established procedure which would have enabled the population to receive a carefully phrased warning of things to come?

Conclusions

"It all began so suddenly, without warning, with no possibility of knowing in time..." Who will ever forget Richard Burton's anguished voice speaking these words as we saw on our screens the first pictures of that catastrophe which fell upon our city, our families and our history, and humbled the civilisation which we had built and which we now shared with all the nations of the world—that overwhelming volume of water blindly destroying what reason had created, sullying all that was dear to us, momentarily stripping us of our courage and our faith...

Like so many others, I relived the tragedy when Zeffirelli's documentary film was televised some three weeks after the flood. And tears sprang to my eyes when I heard those words: "...without warning, with no possibility of knowing in time..."

Florence could have been warned. We must have the courage to face up to that fact. At 8 p.m. on the Thursday, the news of the impending flood could have been quietly circulated among shopkeepers, craftsmen, museum staffs and householders in those areas of the city traditionally subject to flooding. Works of art could have been put out of harm's way; the poor could have carried their humble sticks of furniture to safety; the rich, who had much to save, could have preserved their choicest possessions.

The course of events would have been substantially the same. The city would have been half-buried in mud; people would have suffered hunger and exposure, and doubtless some would have lost their lives. But at least we could have looked forward with some confidence to what the future may bring, twenty years, a hundred years, from now. As it is, to our children and our children's children we leave bitter memories of the flood of November 4th 1966, softened only by the gratitude we feel for the love and help which came to our city from all parts of the world. Of the rest, of the laws and of our rulers, there shall remain nothing but silence.

1. On preceding page.
The Ponte Vecchio at dawn on November 4th

2. The rising waters lifted boats
level with the Lungarno della Zecca Vecchia.
Some of them broke their moorings
and were swept away
through the streets of the town.

3. General view of the river
on the morning of November 4th,
at the height of the flood.

3

2

4. *The flood waters burst into the Piazza Cavalleggeri and invade the Biblioteca Nazionale.*

5. *The torrent of mud and water that poured in upon the treasures of the Biblioteca Nazionale.*

4

5

6. *The arches of the Ponte Vecchio disappeared beneath a raging torrent of water.*

7. *On following page. View of the river at the height of the flood. The water swept through the famous shops on the Ponte Vecchio.*

8. *The Lungarno della Zecca
Vecchia with the river
spilling over into
the heart of the city.*

9. *Via Giotto,
shortly after 10a.m.
The water was travelling
at about 60 k.p.h.*

10. *Wrecked motor-cars
near the Piazza Beccaria.
The wailing of motor horns
rang through the stricken
city as electrical circuits
were completed by the water.*

11. *Piazza Beccaria
invaded by the water.*

10

11

13

14

15

17-18

13, 14, 15. *Piazza Santa Croce.*
Three photographs taken at different times
on November 4th.

16. *A swirling mass of oily water*
in the Via San Giuseppe.
In the background
the apse of Santa Croce.

17, 18. *Outside the basilica of Santa Croce.*
The roofs of motor-cars appear
as the flood waters subside.

19. The flood waters swirling round the Baptistry

20. The Ponte Santa Trinita holding back
the waters of the Arno almost like a dam.
Before long, however, the flood poured
over the embankments and into the streets
below the bridge.

21. *Ponte Santa Trinita. When this photograph was taken the flood waters had begun to subside.*

22. Dawn, November 5th.
The Lungarno Soderini
after the flood.

23. The Ponte Vespucci left covered
with wreckage. In the background
the Cestello church.

24. The shattered Lungarno Acciaioli.
In all, more than a kilometre of embankment
was wrecked by the flood.

25. The Ponte Vecchio viewed across the ruined embankment.

26. A nineteenth century lamp-post swept off its pedestal by the flood but held upright by the deep mud on the embankment. It was some time before street lighting was resumed on the embankments.

26

27

28

29

31

27. Wreckage near
the Via Aretina.

28, 29. More than
ten thousand
motor-cars are thought
to have been destroyed
or damaged by the flood.

30. The Piazza Cavalleggeri
and the Corso dei Tintori,
still flooded on the morning
of November 5th.

31. A ruined bicycle among
the wreckage.

32. *Aerial view of the countryside around Scandicci. Many factories were wrecked in r*

ying industrial areas of the city.

33. *November 5th.*
The mud at the Biblioteca Nazionale.

34. *People picking their way*
through the uprooted cobblestones
outside the Biblioteca Nazionale.

34

35 - 36

35. *Water, mud and wreckage*
in the Borgo Santa Croce.

36. *Piazza Santa Croce.*
Finally boats and light tanks
were able to bring supplies to people
long cut off by the flood.

37. People viewing the
wreckage on the
Ponte Vecchio.

38, 39. The goldsmiths'
shops on the Ponte Vecchio
gutted by the flood waters.

38

40. *Via Barbadori. Paving-stones torn up by the flood.*

41. The first shopkeepers
returning to the Via
Tornabuoni with the street
still deep in oily water.

42. Ghiberti's Porta
del Paradiso.
The fury of the waters
burst open the
Baptistery doors,
which crashed to and fro,
thus loosening the panels.
Miraculously the gate
held firm and
prevented them
from being swept away.

43. Panels of the Porta
del Paradiso dumped
on a barrow.

44. The Palazzo Vecchio
reflected in the
stagnant water
lying in the courtyard
of the Uffizi.

45. *The Lungarno
alle Grazie.*

46. *The sun came out,
but the traces
of mud remained.*

47. *Tree-trunks left
high and dry on the parapet
of the Ponte alle Grazie.*

48. *Motorists inspecting
their wrecked vehicles
in the Corso dei Tintori.*

45

46

47

48

49. *Clearing the mud
out of a house in the
Piazza Mentana.*

50. *Troops at work
in the Piazza Santa Croce.*

51. *The high altar
of the Chiesetta delle Grazie
deep in mud.*

51

52. On preceding page.
The cloister of Santa Croce
under water.

53. Tree-trunks washed up
in the Piazza Santa Croce.

54. The cloister of Santa
Croce after the flood.

55. The interior
of Santa Croce
under a layer of oily mud.

53

54

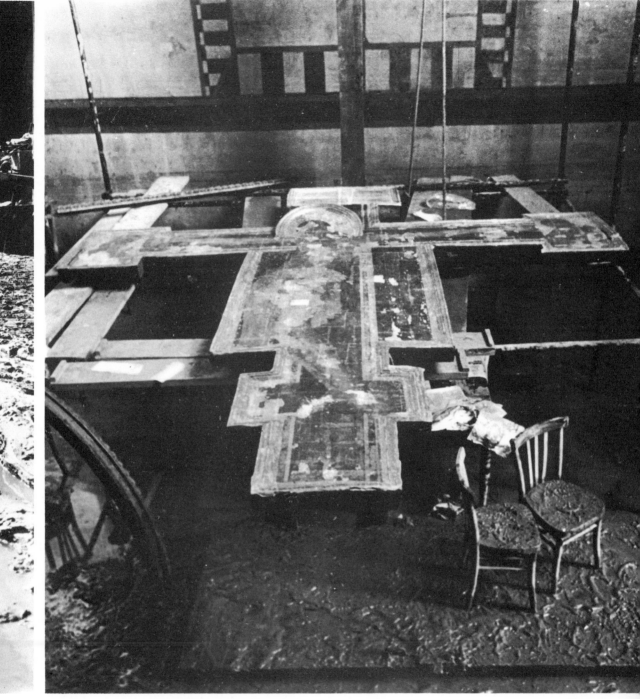

56. *Via Magliabechi after the flood.*

57. *Cimabue's « Crucifixion »*
seventy per cent ruined.
The painting was in the museum of Santa Croce,
which was at one time four metres deep in oily water.
This was the greatest artistic loss of the flood.

58. *Museo dell'Opera del Duomo.*
The wooden models of the Cathedral dome wrecked in the flood.

59. *Clothes and furniture washed out of shops set to dry outside the Palazzo Vecchio.*

60. *The « tide-mark » left by the oil on Bandinelli's marble wall in the chancel of the Cathedral.*

61. *Tanks in the flooded Via Cavour.*

58

59

63

62. *Mud-caked books
in the San Luca chapel,
Chiesa della SS. Annunziata.*

63. *Furnishings and sacred
objects salvaged in the
Chiesa della SS. Annunziata.*

64. *One of the damaged
frescoes by Paolo Uccello
in the cloister of Santa
Maria Novella.*

62

64

65. Shopkeepers
attempting to salvage goods
in the Via Nazionale
near the Stazione Centrale.

66. A bicycle left behind
by the flood.

67. Goldsmiths on the Ponte
Vecchio sifting mud
in the hope of recovering
articles lost in the flood.

69

68. On preceding page. In the days following the flood fresh water was worth its weight in gold.

69. Borgo degli Albizi. People reappear in the streets of the city.

70. Collecting water at the Mercatino di San Piero. In many parts of the city water supplies were cut off for three weeks.

71. People queueing at a food distribution centre.

72. Dismayed citizens viewing the chaos left behind by the flood.

70

73. *Street scene in the Por Santa Maria.*

74. *A young stall-holder*
salvaging souvenirs in the Loggia del Porcellino.

75. The back-breaking
task of clearing out
the cellars...

76. The carcass of a pig
in the Via del Barbadori.
For some days after
the flood there were fears
of an epidemic.

77. A youngster directing
traffic.

78. Via dell'Ariento.
An old workman among his
salvaged possessions.

79. *Loggia del Pesce.*
Many hundreds of antiques
were lost in the flood.

80. *A tailor's dummy*
grotesquely supported
by the chains edging
the pavement in the
Piazza San Giovanni.

81. *A small boy sweeping up outside his father's shop.*

82. *Open-air chemist's— one of several that operated during the emergency, when there was a shortage of medical supplies.*

83, 84. *Soldiers at work in the city centre. Troops played a vital part in combating the 600,000 tons of mud deposited in the city.*

85. *Soldiers break for a meal at Santa Croce.*

83

84

85

86. *Clearing-up operations in the Via Ghibellina.*

87. *The Gavinana district. Old buildings shored up in the Via Gianpaolo Orsini. One of the greatest problems after the floods was that of housing some five thousand stricken families.*

88. *Soldiers at work watched by a small boy.*

86

87

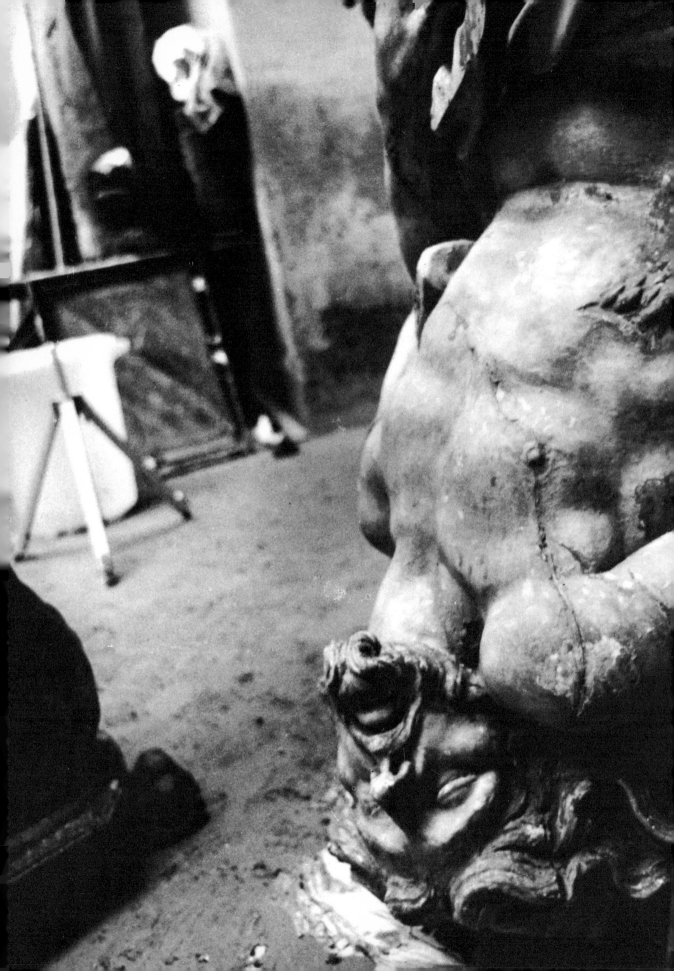

89. *An overthrown statue in the storeroom of the Uffizi's Gabinetto Restauri at the Poste Vecchie.*

90. *A room in the Palazzo Riccardi after the flood.*

91. *The storeroom of the Poste Vecchie: an attempt to restore a fourteenth century painting. In a moving display of solidarity experts hastened to Florence from all parts of the world to assist in the work of restoration.*

90

91

92. *Students at work on the restoration of damaged volumes in the Museo dell'Opera del Duomo.*

93. *A corridor in the Uffizi containing pictures transferred from the flooded parts of the building.*

94. *Museo delle Scienze. Anatomical figures in wax salvaged after the flood.*

95. On preceding page.
Central hall of the Biblioteca
Nazionale with thousands of
volumes ruined by mud.
Young people of all
nationalities helped in the
work of salvage
and restoration.

96. A young woman intent
upon the restoration
of an ancient volume.

97. Students salvaging
books in the Biblioteca
Nazionale.

98. Books caked with mud
in the Biblioteca Nazionale.

99, 100. *About 1,300,000 volumes, as well*
as precious collections of codices and journals,
are believed to have been destroyed or damaged by mud.
It will be many years before the Biblioteca Nazionale
fully recovers from the flood.

101. *Aerial view of flooded countryside west of Florence. Fields remained flooded long after the waters had subsided in the city, and the region's agriculture was severely affected.*

102. *A flooded street at San Donnino near Florence. This village, which is famous for its straw products, was one of the worst hit areas.*

103. *The first relief workers reach San Donnino.*

104. *Two women at the window of their flooded house at San Donnino.*

101

102
103
104

105. *The Arno at the Levane dam.*

106. *Sluice-gates of the Levane dam seen from above. The Florentine magistrature set up an inquiry in an attempt to ascertain what influence the hydroelectric installations of the Valdarno may have had on the flood.*

107. *The Levane dam seen from the front. In the foreground the devastated embankment.*

A menace that has existed for 700 years

"When, in the course of this our mortal life, exceptional and saddening events take place, it is natural that our minds should turn in their perplexity to the history of times past to inquire if happenings of a like kind have ever been recorded. We seek to discover if such past events were more or less calamitous than the present one; we inquire into their causes and effects. If they brought disaster upon mankind, we desire to know what steps were taken to relieve the same, and what diligence was used in hastening those measures likely to lessen the evil effects which would ensue if so unfortunate an accident were ever to be repeated—if indeed there seemed to be no manner of avoiding them completely..."

These words were written in 1845 by Giuseppe Aiazzi in the introduction to his excellent book "Historical Narrations upon the most considerable Floods of the River Arno". It is a lucid and dispassionate little work. Writing today, some 120 years later, we feel neither lucid nor dispassionate. It will be some years before the city's traditional patience and self-sufficiency reassert themselves and calm those feelings of frustration which overtake us whenever we reflect how, for seven centuries and more, Communes, Seignories, Grand Dukes, rulers of all kinds (including many deeply loved by the people), have failed to check the depredations of this unhappy river. As we shall see, it has invariably burst its banks at the same points, for the same reasons, and even in the same dread days of November! (No fewer than three of the greatest floods recorded—those of 1333, 1844 and 1966—have occurred on November 3rd-4th).

With a shrug of the shoulders, those who believe in the existence of supernatural powers seek to explain the phenomenon: "November 3rd and 4th—those are the Devil's days! Following All Saints and All Souls, those festivals so strongly affirming faith in man's survival into a better world, the Devil periodically turns his rage against mankind. He seeks, by spreading grief and destruction, to show that the only reality is earthly reality and to condemn the human race to self-exhaustion and barren paganism." But we do not believe in the Devil...

Like so many of our ancestors, we have seen our city and its people defiled and broken by the flood. We have seen blind men and old folk scraping the mud from their homes; we have seen white-faced young girls slaving hour after hour to salvage what is past repair; we have seen people destitute and stranded, raising their hands to heaven in a plea for bread and water; we have seen the authorities spreading wide their arms in a gesture of dismay and helplessness. And this sort of thing has been going on for seven hundred years.

121

The Sieve becomes swollen, the Arno bursts its banks, floods the Valdarno, carries away the bridges of Florence, and brings disaster to the poor and the weak—those who, in the very nature of things, are the most defenceless. Old people are drowned, humble homes are wrecked, and honest craftsmen are deprived of their livelihood. Profiteers, charitable high-born ladies and a host of engineers and experts come into their own. The authorities fail to meet the challenge, and basic social units emerge from the chaos: the parish priests, the committees of public safety and, today, the local Communist cells. There is heroism and cowardice. Some seek to gain personal advantage by exaggerating the tragedy; others are ready to hush it up. And in this respect the modern mass media are not all that different from the official proclamations of the past.

And we, the heroes of an atom-powered civilisation, lords of a push-button world, view the breakdown of our mechanical slaves first with irritation, then anger, and finally terror. We feel we are being heroic when we walk up the stairs instead of going up in a lift, or when we stand in line for drinking water or half a kilo of salt—but apart from that we feel very much as our ancestors must have felt in centuries gone by. The Arno is the same as it ever was; and so are the defences against the Arno. And so are those who govern us and are responsible for those defences.

Let us look at the old chronicles and examine the facts of the curse that has been hanging over us for seven hundred years.

Devastation once a century

Ferdinando Morozzi da Colle, skilled engineer and "zealous citizen", compiled statistics for Arno floods for the period 1177 to 1761. As can be seen from the table, the river overflowed fifty-four times in the six hundred years. There was a flood of average dimensions every twenty-four years, a major flood every twenty-six years, a very severe flood every hundred years.

Months in which floods occurred	Total	Average floods	Major floods	Very severe floods
January	8	5	3	—
February	2	—	2	—
March	—	—	—	—
April	2	1	1	—
May	2	1	1	—
June	2	2	—	—
July	1	1	—	—
August	1	—	—	1
September . . .	2	1	—	1
October	9	2	6	1
November . . .	12	6	5	1
December . . .	9	2	5	2
Exact months not known for the floods of 1303, 1368, 1538 and 1674	4	4	—	—
	54	25	23	6

The old chronicles

These extracts are from the most celebrated chronicles dealing with historic floods in Florence. Some of the most incisive pages in Villani's works are devoted to this subject, and in 1966 they were reproduced and quoted even in glossy magazines normally dedicated to the private lives and amours of celebrities and royalty. Marchionne di Coppo Stefani, dealing with the same subject as Villani, writes no less vividly and concisely.

THE CHRONICLES OF GIOVANNI VILLANI

BOOK 7 - CHAPTER XXXIV

How there was a great flood which destroyed the Ponte Santa Trinita and the Ponte della Carraia.

In the said year 1269 on the night of the calends of October there was such great rain from heaven that, continuing for two nights and one day, all the rivers of Italy were swollen beyond anything ever seen before. The River Arno burst its bounds so immoderately that a great part of the city of Florence was flooded. Quantities of wood and timber borne by the river were piled up at the foot of the Ponte Santa Trinita, so that the water behind spilled over into the city, where many people were drowned and many buildings were destroyed. At last the force of the water was so great that the bridge collapsed, following which the flow of water and timber crashed against and destroyed the Ponte della Carraia. And when both bridges were fallen in ruins, the level of the water fell, no longer being blocked in its flow, and the flood which had spread through the city began to abate.

BOOK 7 - CHAPTER CXXVI

Of a great flood of water which there was in Florence.

In the said year 1288 on the 5th day of December there was a great rain in Florence and the surrounding countryside, so that the river Arno grew immoderately and overflowed its banks. This continued from morning to night, destroying palaces and buildings near the Ponte Santa Trinita and doing much damage in the country about Florence and Pisa.

BOOK 11 - CHAPTER I

Of a great flood of water in Florence and in almost all of Tuscany.

In the year of Our Lord 1333 on the calends of November, Florence being at that time more powerful and more prosperous than at any time in the century, it pleased God to send His judgement upon our city. That day of All Saints it began to rain in Florence and in the country nearby and in the mountains, and it so continued beyond all known measure for four days and four nights as though the cataracts of heaven were falling. And with the rain came thunder and lightning, and many thunderbolts fell to earth, wherefor all the people were greatly afraid and rang the bells of all the churches in the city, ceasing only when the flood waters rose to a great height. And in their houses people beat upon bowls and cauldrons and cried to God to have mercy on those in peril; and people fled from house to house and from roof to roof, and constructed bridges between houses, and made such noise and tumult that the thunder itself could scarce be heard. With this rain, such abundance of water filled the Arno that it came down with great violence from the mountains and submerged much of the Casentino plain, then all the plain of Arezzo and the upper Valdarno. All was covered with water, which destroyed all the sown crops, broke down and uprooted trees, and invaded and ruined the mills and all but the strongest houses and buildings near the Arno. And thus many people were killed. And as the Arno came down into our plain near Florence it was joined by the Sieve, which was also greatly swollen and had flooded all the Mugello plain; and every ditch which flowed into the Arno was like a river, so that when the Arno reached Florence at nones on Thursday 4th November it overflowed the fields of San Salvi and Bisarno and lay upon them to a depth of six, eight and even ten *braccia*[1]; moreover, the confined passage of the river through the city could in no wise contain so great a flow of water, more particularly since the many weirs serving the mills within the city had caused the bed of the channel to be raised by more than six *braccia*. The depth of the water at the Porta della Croce and the Porta del Renaio was six *braccia* or more, and both of these gates were broken and beaten to the ground. During the first part of that night the wall above the Corso dei Tintori was broken down to a length of one hundred and thirty *braccia* in that part opposite to the dormitory of the friars minor, and thus the

_____

[1] *Braccio* (pl. *braccia*) - a variable measure of length; may here be taken as roughly two feet. [Translator's note].

Arno came more freely into the city; and there was great abundance of water, which first invaded and laid waste the dwelling of the said friars minor and then all that part of the city which lies to the north of the river. The water flooded the streets, to more or less extent, but especially in San Piero Scheraggio and at the Porta San Piero and the Porta del Duomo, and to such degree as the reader shall presently understand from what follows. In the church of San Giovanni the water rose to the top of the altar and to half the height of the columns before the door; and in Santa Reparata to the arch of the old vaults beneath the choir; and it threw down the column bearing the cross with the emblem of San Zanobio that stood in the piazza. At the Palazzo del Popolo it rose to the first step of the flight before the door in the Via di Vaccherecqia, which is among he highest points of the city; and there were six *braccia* in the lower court of the Palazzo del Comune. At the Abbey of Florence it reached the foot of the high altar, and the same in Santa Croce. In Orto San Michele and the Mercato Nuovo it rose two *braccia*, and the same in the Mercato Vecchio, and over all that part of the town. To the south of the river there was great depth of water, and especially in San Niccolò, Borgo Pidiglioso, Borgo San Friano and Camaldoli, with great ruin to the poor and humble people who lived in low houses; and it extended to the piazza and along Via Maggio almost to San Felice. And that said Thursday at the hour of vespers the force of the water broke down the weir of Ognissanti and in two places battered down the city wall behind San Friano, to a length of more than five hundred *braccia*. And the guard tower upon that wall was twice struck by lightning and almost wholly destroyed. And with the breaking of the said weir of Ognissanti the Ponte alla Carraia incontinently collapsed and fell, except for two arches on the northern side of the river. And then, too, fell the Ponte da Santa Trinita, except for one pile and one arch on the side of the church; and the Ponte Vecchio, which was beaten by the wood and débris carried by the Arno, was overcome by the fierce water, and the houses and shops which stood upon it were ruined, and at last all collapsed and there remained but two of the piles in the centre. And at the Ponte Rubaconte the Arno passed over the side arches and broke its banks and penetrated into many parts of the town. The water destroyed the palace of the Altafronte castle and many of the houses along the river between the said castle and the Ponte Vecchio. And there fell into the Arno the statue of Mars which was upon a pillar at the foot of the Ponte Vecchio on the northern side. The ancients said, and left their words in writing, that when the statue should fall or be moved Florence would undergo great danger. And this was said with good reason, as experience has proved and as this chronicle will show. Mars fell, and as many houses as there were between the Ponte Vecchio and the Ponte dalla Carraia, and

all along the Arno as far as the millrace was devastated; and it was the same in Borgo San Iacopo and in all the streets along the Arno on both sides, where there was ruin and chaos; and similarly many ill-founded houses were destroyed in many other parts of the city. The following night the force of the water broke down the wall at Ognissanti to a length of four hundred and fifty *braccia*, and this diminished the quantity of water which lay within the city and was still increasing; so that though the city had been in great peril, the water returned impetuously to the Arno through the breach in the wall above-mentioned and left all the streets and the ground-floor shops and homes and the cellars, which are so numerous in Florence, full of evil-smelling mud. And more than six months passed before all this was cleansed away. Moreover, almost all the wells in Florence were ruined and had to be remade. To the west of the city the Arno flooded the flat country of Legnaia, Ognano, Settimo, Ormannoro, Campi, Brozzi, Sammoro, Peretola and Micciole, as far as Signa, and also about Prato, laying the fields under great depth of water, destroying vines, and sweeping away houses and mills, many people and almost all the cattle. Beyond Montelupo and Capraia it continued so, the Arno being joined by many other rivers which were also greatly swollen and had broken the bridges which spanned them. To the same degree the Arno covered and laid waste the lower Valdarno, and Pontormo and Empoli and Santa Croce and Castelfranco, ruining the walls of those towns in great measure, and all the low-lying land of Samminiato and Fucecchio and Montetopoli and Marti al Pontadera. And when it reached Pisa it would have flooded all had it not overflowed and carved for itself a new path to the sea; and on the other side of Pisa it joined itself with the river Serchio. But this notwithstanding, great part of Pisa was flooded, and great damage was caused to the flat country of Valdiserchio and around the city. But in subsiding, the waters deposited even as much as two *braccia* depth of soil upon the land, which was of great utility to the population thereabouts. This flood brought great tribulation to the city and country of Florence, killing some three hundred people, men, women and children, (though at first the number was thought to be three thousand). And great numbers of cattle were lost; and bridges, houses and mills were destroyed in great number, so that not one bridge was spared in all the country of Florence. And much merchandise was lost, and woollen cloth, and tools and furniture besides; and casks were broken, so that great quantity of wine went to waste. The same can be said of grain and forage; while such crops as had been sown were destroyed, and fields were ruined and laid waste. And as the low-lying lands were flooded and spoilt, so the hills and slopes were rent and torn and the good earth was carried from them by the waters. So that I, who saw all these things, could in no wise estimate in money the damage that was wrought; but in the city of Florence alone the re-making of bridges, walls and streets cost more than one hundred and fifty thousand gold florins. And such destruction was not peculiar to Florence and its country alone, albeit the disorderly abundance of the Arno there caused the worst damage; but every river in Tuscany and Romagna became swollen in like manner, destroying bridges and flooding the countryside, as did the River Tiber; and great damage was caused at Borgo a San Sepolcro, Castello, Perugia, Todi, Orbivieto and Rome, and also in the countries of Siena and Arezzo, and in the Maremma. It is known that on the day of the flood and for many days afterwards there was great shortage of flour and bread in Florence for the destruction of the mills and bakehouses; but the people of Pistoia, Prato, Colle and Poggibonizzi and many other towns sent generous abundance of bread and flour to Florence, which was in great need. It was a question for old inhabitants of good memory which was the greater flood—this, or the one which took place in the year of Our Lord 1269. Most said that the ancient flood had scarcely less quantity of water, but that this time the city was worse flooded and the damage was greater; and this because of the improvidence of the authorities in allowing those who owned mills along the river to construct weirs, which had raised the bed of the Arno by as much as seven *braccia*; but God ever sends folly to those He will undo. And afterwards it was at once decreed that there should be no weir or mill within the limits of the bridges, nor for two thousand *braccia* above Rubaconte, nor for four thousand *braccia* below the Ponte dalla Carraia. This order was given, and officers were appointed to supervise the rebuilding of bridges and walls. But to return to the argument broached above, we believe this flood to have been much greater than the ancient one, in that there was not rain alone, but also earthquake. Certain it is that water sprang forth from the earth in many places, and even in the mountains; and therefore have we recounted of this flood the more fully, that it may ever be remembered; for no such adversity and damage came upon the city of Florence since that time it was destroyed by Totila, the Scourge of God.

HISTORY OF FLORENCE
BY MARCHIONNE
DI COPPO STEFANI

BOOK 7

How there was a great flood of water, which brought great damage to the city and to the inhabitants.

In the year of Our Lord MCCCXXXIII on the first day of November it began to rain so strongly and with such quantity of water that the rivers and ditches flowing into the Arno were greatly swollen; and on the third day of November the plain of Arezzo and the upper Valdarno were flooded and many buildings were destroyed. And on the night of that same day the Porta alla Croce and the Porta alla Giustizia were broken down, together with the wall of the Corso de' Tintori, so that with the great flow of water three parts of the city were flooded, and the people were greatly afraid. The church of the friars minor was flooded, and in the piazza of the said friars, at the highest point, there lay six *braccia* of water; and it continued through that place and the Porta di Duomo and as far as the altar of San Giovanni. And the water flooded the church of Santa Reparata and threw down a column bearing a cross which had been set there where San Zenobio worked a miracle, before the north door of San Giovanni. And it flooded the Campo Corbolino and the piazza of Santa Maria Novella and the Mercato Vecchio; and in the Mercato Nuovo there were three *braccia* of water; and in the Palazzo del Popolo the water came to the second staircase, and in the Podesta there lay five *braccia* in the courtyard; and the flood grew with great violence and struck down the Ponte Vecchio, and raged through the main street from the Porta a San Gallo to the Porta a San Piero Gattolino. And the Ponte a Santa Trinita, by which one passes from the church to the Via Maggio, and the Ponte alla Carraia, by which one passes from the Borgo Ognissanti, and many houses along the Arno between the Altafronte castle and the Ponte a Santa Trinita were all destroyed. Almost all the mills along the Arno were destroyed, as were those which were mounted upon ships; and men and women and children were carried away; and the citizens saw no way of escape, but fled from house to house and from roof to roof. And to the south of the river great part of Borgo a San Niccolò and all of Camaldoli were flooded. And if, to the north of the river, the waters had not broken down the wall at Ognissanti, they would have risen yet higher within the city; but with the breaking of the said wall they began to subside. From nones until evening on the Thursday the flood was at its height; and with darkness it began to decline. In the lower Valdarno there was great loss of life; many cattle were lost, and there was great destruction of houses and furniture. Sown crops were ruined, and good tilled land was damaged. Great harm befell the walls of towns in the Valdarno, even as far as Pisa; and within Pisa the flood wrought damage. But many lands were improved by the depositing of soil carried by the water, in some places to a depth of two *braccia*; and many bogs and ponds were filled with the earth that was so deposited. Old people said that never in their time had there been such great quantity of water; and all the people of Italy regretted the damage that had been done in Florence and the loss of merchandise, (which was inestimable), except the

Cardinal, who rejoiced, saying that all had been done by God in return for the damage which Holy Church had suffered in Ferrara at the hands of the Florentines; little did he know that Florence would soon laugh and rejoice once more at his new afflictions.

From a manuscript diary of Father Vincenzo Fineschi.

On the fourth day of November 1333, which was a Thursday, there came a great flood upon all the city and plain of Florence, and many Good Christians were killed. Many beasts were drowned, and palaces, towers and houses without number were destroyed; lands were laid waste, and great number of farms damaged beyond measure. The which flood at first destroyed the Ponte alla Carraia and the Ponte di Santa Trinita and the Ponte Vecchio and other dignities of Florence too numerous to mention, and which few would believe if they had not seen with their own eyes.

The flood of August 1547

Perhaps more than any other, the flood of August 1547 aroused thoughts of the "Wrath of God". It took everyone by surprise—even today the Arno in August appears to be a singularly unexciting river; and it struck with amazing speed, a hundred deaths and an immense amount of damage resulting from a mere three hours of flooding.

Even in those far-off days, however, Bernardo Segni (the second of the authors cited below) was able to conclude his account of the flood with these words: "In these ways man had contributed to the disaster—while the sins of mankind were held to be responsible for the intervention of divine judgement... And these frequent floods were certainly a presage of future and yet more serious disasters which might come upon us and which might finally bring sense to the Tuscan province, whose governors are devoid of intelligence and whose citizens lack authority, not only in Florence but also in Siena..."

STORY OF HIS TIMES BY GIO. BATISTA ADRIANI

Book 6 (1547)

At this time there came a very great flood, which covered a large part of the city; and this was all the more remarkable as such inordinate rain is by no means to be expected at that season of the year. At nine o'clock in the evening on 12th August a great rain began in Florence. Carried by the winds over the Mugello, it extended even to the mountains of Vernio, and was so heavy and so persistent throughout that night that people said they had never seen the like. Within a short time all the brooks and streams of the Mugello were carrying a great weight of water into the Sieve, breaking down and uprooting trees and devastating mills and houses close to the river. In a few hours the water rose many *braccia* in the flat country near the Sieve and caused much damage, and it came upon Ponte a Sieve with such violence that it swept away the bridge and destroyed mills and houses, as well as the Franciscan church. Many people were drowned, having no time to escape, in as much as the disaster came upon them by night and was in no way expected. So great was the flood that, in some places it was forty *braccia* from the bed of the river to the surface of the water; and

from this one can imagine the magnitude of the tempest. The beasts of the field were carried away, and nothing that the flood reached was spared; vineyards and orchards were completely laid waste. The water came down with such fury that it reached the walls of Florence before any suspected its approach. In the fields of San Salvi it rose to more than ten *braccia* and came to the Porta alla Croce shortly after noon on 13th August. Finding the gate open, it entered with great violence, breaking down low walls, flooding all the area that was flat and bringing great quantities of mud and débris into the city. In the Piazza Santa Croce it covered the steps before the church and was equally deep in all that district. Two hundred and fifty *braccia* of river bank were broken down between the Ponte Rubaconte and the Ponte Vecchio, and so much water overflowed that the corn market was submerged in a moment and all the flour and fodder were ruined. And it advanced and flooded the offices beneath the Palazzo Pubblico so swiftly that the clerks had no time to save the documents, many of which were lost. It then spread through other parts of the city, and great damage was caused. The quarter of Santa Croce was devastated, and it was, in short, the greatest flood that men had yet seen in this century. In the Mugello and from Ponte a Sieve to the city, no fewer than a hundred people lost their lives, and sixty bodies were later found upon the shore. At the same time the Bisenzio was also causing damage in its valley, and so were all the other rivers taking their origin in the mountains which enclose the Mugello, so that even the Romagna, beyond those mountains, suffered from flooding. And this year there was much rain throughout Italy. The horror of the flood lasted no more than three hours in Florence, and the city was left filthy and much encumbered with mud and débris, so that the authorities had to take action; and such were the speed, industry and care of the people that the city was clean and returned to its former beauty within a few days. This great flood, coming at such a season, deeply moved all men, and the people asked themselves if God meant thereby to give warning of some yet greater evil to come.

HISTORY OF FLORENCE
BY BERNARDO SEGNI

BOOK XII

In the month of August 1547 there was in Florence a great and sudden flood, greater than any there had been for two hundred and fifty years in that city. The waters rose in the corn market to a height of eight *braccia*, and all the quarter of Santa Croce was flooded. Many houses were then ruined, their foundations being weakened by the water. It was said that the flood caused damage to the sum of three hundred thousand *scudi* in the city and the country nearby; and this could well be surpassed by some future flood arising out of the same causes. And even before this time great damage had been suffered because the high rainfall had in a measure changed and raised the bed of the river; so that all the other rivers emptying into it could scarce be accomodated and at each rain overflowed their banks and did great harm to the fertile land near them. The wealth of the province had thus been much diminished, especially in the low-lying areas. Nor did there seem to be any hope of alleviating this problem, for though the Duke took an interest in these matters, the engineers he employed to work on the rivers, (at great expense), always finished by worsening conditions rather than improving them. It was well known that the water coming into the Arno from the Chiane had done great harm. Antonio da Ricasoli had drained and taken possession of large areas around Arezzo, and the marshy water so drained off had carried much soil into the river and raised its bed not a little. And others said, perhaps with better reason, that because very great numbers of trees had been cut down for timber in the Falterona and other mountains, the soil was more easily loosened by water and carried down to silt up the beds of rivers. In these ways man had contributed to the disaster—while the sins of mankind were held to be responsible for the intervention of divine judgement. Those same sins were believed to be the true origin, not only of the damage wrought by the rivers of our province, but also of every other error, misgovernment or fatal custom indulged in by princes to the detriment of their people. And these frequent floods were certainly a presage of future and yet more serious disasters which might come upon us and which might finally bring sense to the Tuscan province, whose governors are devoid of intelligence and whose citizens lack authority, not only in Florence but also in Siena.

MOROZZI
OF THE ANCIENT
AND MODERN CONDITION
OF THE RIVER ARNO

PART I (1547)

In the manuscript diary of Marucelli it is recorded, amongst other things, that the river banks were submerged and could no longer be seen, that the water came to the corner of Monte Loro, (di Candeli), and that three trees and other timber were cast up at the Porta di San Pulinari. Three chapels were destroyed in the church of San Simone, and three huge beams were left before the door of this church. A huge walnut-tree was deposited in the piazza of San Firenze, and another tree, together with a fig and an olive, was cast up on the Ponte Vecchio. In San Niccolò and in some other parts of the city the water rose to six and even seven *braccia*. The following record of this flood is to be found in the General Archives of this city of Florence:

"Thirteenth day of August 1547.

"I record that on the above day at about the hour of noon the Arno flooded the quarter of Santa Croce, from the Piazza de' Signori to the Pazzi and to San Piero and Borgo Pinti, and other districts such as Santa Trinita, Ognissanti and, south of the river, San Niccolò. The water entered through the door into the Gabella de' Contratti, where I was working, and there rose to a height of two and a half *braccia*; and at my home, at the Canto alla Briga, there was a like amount of water. Many walls were broken down, as were 120 *braccia* of the river bank, and great numbers of houses were damaged. And the river overflowed at Pontassieve, doing great damage in the country, sweeping away whole houses and drowning one family in its entirety. So that the authorities reckoned the damage to bridges alone at one hundred thousand *scudi*; and in all the country of Florence the damage amounted to more than one million in gold, the like of which had not been seen in many years".

BALDINUCCI
OF THE LIFE
OF BARTOLOMMEO AMMANNATI

(1557)

On the twelfth day of September there came a ruinous rain which so increased the volume of the river that it began to overflow in the Casentino and below, destroying mills and other buildings, sweeping away bridges, and drowning many of the inhabitants in those parts. Towards Dicomano, at the foot of the mountains, streams and ditches emptied such great flow of water into the Sieve that all the Mugello valley was flooded; and there, too, much harm was caused by the waters. When the Sieve joined with the Arno, the water came down with great violence upon our city, and this was at about the third hour of the day. It first destroyed the Ponte a Santa Trinita, whose ruins there caused the river to rise beyond measure, so that it overflowed the banks and flooded almost all the plain of the city. At the same time two arches of the Ponte alla Carraia were broken and carried away, and all the embankment fell between the Ponte Vecchio and the Ponte Rubaconte, and almost all the city's gardens were flooded. Among these was the one between the Zecca Vecchia and the convent of the Fanciulle del Ceppo, but recently reconstructed by Duke Cosimo and bearing his arms and this inscription, (which may also be seen elsewhere in the city): COSMUS MEDICES DIRUENTE ARNO INSTAURAVIT. A.D.M.D.L. VII. Over the level ground at the Porta alla Croce the water passed with such violence that it threw down the timber and iron fittings that barred the gate and in its first fury destroyed a house. The city having been thus invaded, there remained scarce any part of it that was not flooded. In some places the waters rose to nine and ten *braccia*, inspiring the population with a fear which the reader may well imagine. This disaster came about at a time when, all the fields being worked, the water was able to carry off a great amount of soil, which filled cellars and the ground-floor rooms of houses, so that infinite quantities of foodstuffs were lost and many buildings collapsed; and so that those areas which were flooded, being about two thirds of Florence, could not afterwards be recognised. And it was the opinion of some that this flood was in no way inferior to that of 1333, though others believed the contrary, the level of the ground, as they said, having much risen during the intervening years. And the great quantity of earth which remained in the houses and churches of the city was later, at great expense and under the direction of Ammannati, who had been made the Duke's engineer, removed and used to make the embankments which are to be seen piled against the inner face of the city walls. And these embankments are so high that one of those inscriptions — made of white marble and bearing the Lily (arms of the city), and the Cross,

(arms of the people and the Guelph party), the date 1310, and listing the legal width of streets, heights of walls and breadth of the defensive ditch—may be seen almost level with the surface of the ground. And this inscription is beneath an arch at an angle of the wall between the Porta alla Croce and the Porta a Pinti; whereas in other places, such as in the Via della Scala, inscriptions of this kind are to be found high above the ground. The city of Florence being divided into two parts by the River Arno, the destruction of the bridges obliged people for many months either to walk a great distance to the Ponte Vecchio, which had remained intact, or to cross the water in much discomfort by boat. Wherefor Duke Cosimo, seeking to remedy such inconvenience, had two arches of the Ponte alla Carraia rebuilt in the year 1559; and the foundations were begun on the eighth day of August. He likewise ordained that the Ponte di Santa Trinita should be reconstructed; and this noble enterprise was entrusted to Ammannati. He made a wondrous model of the bridge, and when all was ready for the work and all the materials had been gathered together, the foundations were begun in March 1566. It was observed that the destruction of the bridges in 1269 and 1557 had resulted from the quantity of wood and timber carried by the flood; the which, blocking the arches of the bridges, had led to the water overflowing into the city, (bringing death and ruin to the inhabitants), and to great increase in pressure against the structure of the said bridges, whose piles and arches were so constructed that great resistance was offered to the progress of the waters. The Duke now made a prudent law forbidding cut wood and timber to be kept anywhere in the country within so many *braccia* of the river bank; while Ammannati skilfully constructed the piles of the new bridge with strong stone and very sharp angles, so that the current might thus be readily divided and the waters enabled to pass swiftly and freely. And yet more wonderful was it that he made the arches very flat, so that even at the sides of the said arches the aperture was wide and open. And with this clever invention he gave the bridge incomparable lightness and grace, and also great strength, as has been shown by the experience of more than a hundred years. Not only has the bridge itself safely withstood great floods, but it has also, by allowing free passage to the water, helped to preserve both the Ponte Vecchio and the Ponte Rubaconte from danger.

SCIPIONE AMMIRATO
TO DON VIRGINIO ORSINO,
DUCA DI BRACCIANO

(1589)

It rained continuously through the last days of October, so that, on the Monday evening, the penultimate day of that month, it began to be suspected that the river might overflow. For all that, however, there were but few who privately determined to make preparation for a flood. But at about the fifth hour word spread through the city, particularly in those parts near the river, that the flood waters were approaching, so that many people rose and began to clear the lower parts of their houses, board up their doors and windows, look to the safety of their wine, and make such preparations as they were able to in the time remaining. Between seven and eight o'clock the river overflowed its banks in many places and poured through the lower parts of the city on both sides of the Arno. It is common opinion, based upon the damage caused by the river in the upper Valdarno, that if the water had been able to enter the city through the Porta di San Niccolò and the Porta alla Croce, as happened in '57, the flood would have risen as high or even higher than it did in that year. Whether or not that may have been so, it is certain that the river, entering first by way of the drains and then by way of the houses which extend from the Fortezza Vecchia to the banks of the Arno, flooded the whole of the Santa Croce quarter. It ran from the Cestello, San Pier Maggiore and the corner of the Pazzi to the steps of the Badia, (without touching the Borgo degli Albizi), and on to the Palazzo de' Gondi, where it covered the low wall, and the Dogana, and towards San Piero Scheraggio, occupying all that lay between there and the Arno. I have given Your Excellency this list of places so that, by drawing a line through them, you may understand that all between them and the river was under water. The river also overflowed by way of the shops beneath the Corridore and over all the bank between the Ponte Vecchio and the Ponte della Carraia, the water reaching the Via Vacchereccia, Porta Santa Maria, Borgo Sant'Apostolo and Santa Trinita, and almost to the Palazzo degli Strozzi. It occupied the Via Parione and Via della Vigna and, overflowing with great violence near the Ponte alla Carraia and through the houses along the river, entered the Borgo d'Ogni Santi and filled all that area, together with the Via del Moro and the Via de' Federighi, where mountains of mud and débris were deposited. No little fear was aroused in that quarter by a large beam which beat against the side door of the Palazzo de' Ricasoli and broke it down, so that the water, pouring through this door and the one which gives straight onto the Via d'Ogni Santi, was like a great river. Swiftly it flowed towards the Porta del Prato, but found that gate closed and therefore returned and spread through the Via di Palazzuolo and almost to the Via della Scala. This was the extent of the flood on this side of the Arno. Much the same occurred to the south of the river, except that the hill prevented the spreading of the waters. The Via de' Renai was flooded, as was the Via de' Bardi, where much water entered by way of a drain. The Via de' Guicciardini was not touched, but the water flowed up the Borgo San Iacopo and without an obstacle to the Porta a San Friano; and finding that gate closed, it turned into all the side streets, to a greater or lesser degree according to the level of the ground, so that almost all of Camaldoli was flooded, and the poverty of the inhabitants was such that there was great suffering. With the light of day, it was found that a number of horses belonging to Your Highness and to members of the Court had been drowned in the stables beneath the Magistrati; and many more would have been drowned but for the diligence of the men responsible. It seems, however, that by the Grace of God there were only two people killed in all the city—a goldsmith and a serving-woman who had descended to a cellar to save some wine and had no time to escape the violent invasion of the water. I blush to tell Your Excellency of the misadventure which befell Your Excellency's whitewasher, for it will appear that, among the remembrances of events far from amusing, I have sought matter for jest; and yet what I have to tell is the whole truth. This man had in his shop, (which is at the steps of the Badia), a large tub of whitewash which, when the water approached it, began, as lime always does, to smoke and crackle; and, some baskets being nigh, there began a fire. The alarm was at once given in the Palazzo del Bargello opposite, and the guard ran and broke down the door with their axes and brought help to the whitewasher, who, cut off from the rest of his house by the flood, had never dreamed that his baskets would catch fire at a time when the city was all but under water. The great anxiety that now affected the people of Florence was that the river showed no sign of subsiding, nor the weather of changing, even after the quantity of rain that had already fallen. And seeing the river bearing dead oxen, chests and even a bed, the population feared that there might come another and even greater flood. And, indeed, at ten o'clock at night a second flood wave did come down, with no less violence than the first—an occurrence most rare in the records of the city. And all the Tuesday and the following night passed in pain and anguish, and many affirm that there was yet a third flux at the third hour. As it was learnt later, the river grew for the first time as a result of the flood waters of the Sieve, which, if they had come down with the main flood of the Arno, (as normally happens), would without fail have brought about the same effects as in 1333 and 1557. The law made by Grand Duke Cosimo proved most effective, and the only wood carried down to the city was that which the flood itself had been able to uproot. Of great utility likewise was that buttress constructed at the Lungarno della Zecca, compressing the flow of water as does the neck of a bottle and so in great measure lessening its impetus. But outside the city, and especially at Incisa and in the Casentino, there was great damage to fields, and mills and houses were ruined, and cattle swept away; and a goodly number of people were killed. So that many reckon, all things considered, that the damage amounted to as much as one million—which, for myself, I can scarce believe. From below the city it is believed that the whole of Pisa would have been flooded, had not the main flow of the water turned aside into the great ditch before reaching so far. There is constant talk of a wondrous event that came about in the upper Valdarno, not far from Montevarchi. A number of poor country folk had taken refuge from the flood in some willow-trees, and among them there was a woman who, whether from fear or because her hour had genuinely come, began there to experience the pains of labour. And her own courage and the Grace of God gave her strength so that, though in constant danger of falling to her death and with, before her eyes, the spectacle of companions in less sturdy trees being swept away by the flood, she bore her pains and gave birth to a child. And she lived thereafter; and the child might have lived also, but that there was no help to be got, so that it died of cold and privation among those same waters that had seen it come to life. As Your Excellency must know, the Grand Duke was at Poggio. It was his desire to come to Florence, and as he could by no means travel there directly across country, he determined to go first to Prato; and though everyone sought to dissuade him, he boarded a boat and came to Prato with no other company than Signor Di Giovanni, Sig. Cammillo del Monte, Sig. Gio. Vincenzo Vitelli, Sig. Marchese di Bagno, Signor Biagio, the Chamberlain and one page. He there gave orders for many loads of bread to follow him, and got into a coach drawn by three horses and came with great difficulty to Florence. He came to the stables and personally gave order that horses should be got ready, as many as there were men in his company, and then went to the Nunziata to pray. Thence he passed to the Murate and to the convents of Monticelli, Montedomini, San Francesco and Capitolo, which, being in low-lying places, had suffered grievously; and he caused bread, wine and money to be given to all, and he comforted them and gave them courage, promising that men and help would be sent to them. Having seen all of this quarter, he passed over the Ponte Rubaconte to visit the Borgo San Niccolò and Camaldoli, where he ordered that the poor folk should be helped in the same way as the convents. Thence he crossed the Ponte alla Carraia and came to the Porta al Prato; and in short he visited all parts of the city, performing good offices for the religious houses and for the poor wherever they were to be found. And I can assure Your Excellency—and may I die for an ingrate and a bad Christian if I do not speak in all sincerity—that I never in my life saw anything more noble than the Grand Duke Ferdinand as, with no guard and accompanied by few horsemen and fewer still on foot, he went about the city performing the true offices of a prince.

In Florence, this fifteenth day of November 1589.

GIUSEPPE AIAZZI
REPORT UPON THE FLOODING
OF THE RIVER ARNO
3rd NOVEMBER 1844

It is foolhardy, perhaps, to attempt a description of how the River Arno without warning overflowed its banks, flooded the streets, squares and houses of much of our city, and brought sudden terror to the population. Mere words can paint no true picture of the many tragic scenes which we have witnessed. Yet, as our forebears made sorrowful record of the damage wrought by the great floods of the past, so we will boldly attempt to pass down to future generations some account of the disaster which Eternal Providence has but lately visited upon us.

The autumn passed agreeably until the middle of October, with warm weather and clear skies, and there seemed good hope that it would so continue. Vain hope indeed! For at that time the Sirocco began to blow, and with it came rain. At first it rained intermittently, but later it continued without a break for many days and nights on end—and so heavily that the saturated earth could not absorb the water, which poured down into the plain by way of ditches and gullies, uprooting trees and hedges and dislodging great quantities of soil. The streams thus swollen flowed into the larger tributaries, which could no longer contain the great quantity of water. They burst their banks, and the flood poured down over a broad front towards the Arno, sweeping away bridges and breaking down walls and embankments which were designed to control the flow of water. The turbulent flood continued, and great damage was done to the fertile lands of the Casentino, around Arezzo, and in the Chiane and the upper Valdarno—so that any full account of the havoc caused in those provinces would be an endless tale of sorrow and desolation.

The Sieve, which joins the Arno only ten miles above Florence, grew swiftly and immoderately, and many people consider that this river was once again the main cause of the disaster which came upon us. Before reaching Dicomano, it cuts across the centre of the Mugello from west to east, gathering all the water flowing down from the mountains which enclose that province; and on this occasion it overflowed its banks and ruined all the flourishing and carefully cultivated fields and swept away the new bridge to which it had given its name. It then destroyed many houses and buildings which stood in its path, and uprooted trees, and carried off cattle and great quantities of furniture and foodstuffs belonging to poor peasants and labourers, who, seeing themselves deprived in a moment of the fruits of years of toil, would have dared all to wrest back their humble possessions from the flood. The flood not only destroyed the property of these unfortunate inhabitants, but also denied them the hope of being able to make good their losses for many years to come. For it will be a long time before the fields are cleared of the stones and sand deposited by the waters and can again be sown—and even longer before the new vines and fruit-trees begin to yield so well as those which have been destroyed. The terrible current then descended into the plain of Florence, where it joined with the River Arno, which, being thus almost doubled in size and fury, overflowed its banks and all the walls which had been built to defend those fields that constitute the charm and delight of Ripoli, Rovezzano and San Salvi. It tore up trees by the roots and destroyed the vegetables in which those plains abound at every season, covering everything deep in sand, so that what had been a vast and scrupulously cared-for garden was transformed almost overnight into a gloomy, sterile desert.

As it had devastated the rustic dwellings and fields mentioned above, so it struck down the iron bridge that spanned the Arno above the weir at the Zecca Vecchia and, early on Sunday 3rd November, burst into Florence by the Porta alla Croce and the Porta di San Niccolò, which thus apeared more like cataracts than city gates. Neither the gates nor the roads on either side of them were passable for many days. The water then began to spread through a large part of the city, first bursting from the drains and sewers which debouch into the Arno, then flooding high over the river banks at many points. It was fortunate that all this came about at an hour when many citizens were leaving their homes to go to church or to do the day's shopping, for they saw the water rising and were able to warn those who were still in bed and at home and had no idea that danger was approaching. But for this, many poor people living in single-storey houses in the low-lying parts of the city could well have been drowned. How many mothers there were who had left their dear children quietly sleeping at home in order to attend divine service—and now found themselves prevented by the flood from returning to rescue or to perish with their little ones! The churches of Sant'Ambrogio, San Giuseppe, Santa Croce, San Simone, San Remigio, San Iacopo tra' Fossi, San Firenze, Santi Apostoli, Santa Trinita, Ognissanti and San Niccolò echoed with their prayers and lamentations—and with those of many fathers who had come out for the same devout purpose or for the no less sacred task of procuring food for their dependents and could now return to their loved ones only at the risk of their own lives. In tearful chorus they besought the Holy Mother to take their innocent children under Her protection. And if these were the feelings of those who were unable to return to their families, we can easily imagine the condition of people who were trapped in their houses, consumed with anxiety for dear ones who had but recently gone forth.

It would be a never-ending task to list the quantities of foodstuffs that were lost, especially corn, wine and oil, with the flooding of ground floors and cellars, both of merchants and of private citizens. Casks and jars were dashed against walls and ceilings and smashed by the fury of the invading waters, and the precious contents were scattered and lost.

The destructive flow of water made its way before long into the large store-rooms beneath the Uffizi, where the Dogana, for the convenience of merchants, keep goods imported into the city. The chaos there was indescribable, as the rarest manufactured goods and most precious foodstuffs, (which had been imported from beyond the seas and mountains in return for our most valuable gold), were mishandled by the waters and reduced to ruin. Cases, casks and sacks were torn asunder, and sugar, coffee, spices and medicines, dye-stuffs and other liquids were mixed together into a foul sea of mud, upon which floated articles of every description; so that this rich and spacious store-house appeared like a loathsome rubbish pit, in which some evil genius had delighted to throw everything into confusion and produce the greatest possible disorder. Never again can Heaven inflict such a deplorable and heart-rending spectacle upon suffering mankind—terrifying as it was to the eyes of the hardiest and most fearless observers.

It would be heart-breaking to compile a complete record of the devastation caused by this accursed flood, and the result of such labour would be no more than a repetition of doleful narratives set down by our ancestors following similar disasters—the details of which we are now remembering as though to console ourselves in our present tribulation. And if, compared with past floods, we have few human victims to mourn, this may be attributed to the hour at which the waters came upon us rather than to their being less violent than those of times past. Indeed, this flood was scarcely, if at all, inferior to that of 1740, which is traditionally remembered among us as being great beyond measure. As in 1740, this time, too, Florence and the surrounding countryside and the whole of the lower Valdarno almost to the gates of Pisa remained under water for several days. Wherefor, " ... like one who, breathless, has attained the shore and turns to gaze upon the perilous deep ", I will limit myself to mentioning the extreme points of the flood's extent and leave the reader to imagine for himself the streets and squares deep in water which, according to the slope of the ground, either impetuously followed the course of the main current or swirled dangerously to find its own level among the cellars and basements of nearby buildings.

On the right bank of the Arno, then, the waters poured down the Borgo la Croce to the Piazza di Sant'Ambrogio, where they all but crossed the threshold of the church. From there they branched out into four main streams, down the Via de' Pentolini, Via Pietra piana, Via di Mezzo and Via de' Pilastri, whence they extended to half way up Cafaggiolo and, by a side road, to the steps of Santa Maria Maddalena. From the Piazzetta della Zecca Vecchia they came along the Via delle Poverine, Via delle Torricelle and Corso de' Tintori to the Piazza di San Iacopo tra' Fossi and the Piazza di Santa Croce; the first spread from San Giuseppe in every direction, and the others, by way of Borgo Santa Croce and Via de' Benci, came together again in that piazza, covering the posts which encircle it. From this piazza, the waters which had flowed into it from many directions began to find their own level, following the slope of the streets leading out of it, flooding them in all directions, so that, by the direct course of the flood and the other roads to the north, they joined up with those of the Via de' Pilastri; and to the west, following a line from Candeli, via the Borgo Pinti, the arch and market of San Piero, the Piazza di San Simone and Piazza de' Peruzzi, they met up in many places with those coming down from the Piazza delle Travi; whence they flooded two thirds of the Via della Ninna, between the southern side of the Palazzo Vecchio and the Uffizi, and on the other side, having covered the Piazza di San Firenze, they invaded the Via de' Balestrieri to some way past the door of the Presidenza del Buon Governo.

From the Piazza del Granduca, the Uffizi, Via Vacchereccia and Via Por Santa Maria, the water gushing from drains and flowing over the embankment between the Ponte Vecchio and the Ponte di Santa Trinita towards the Palazzo Strozzi flooded the Borgo Santi Apostoli, and the Via delle Terme and the narrow streets which lead into it. The water flowed down the alleys leading off the embankment between the Ponte di Santa Trinita and the Ponte della Carraia and flooded all of Parione, Vigna Nuova, Via dei Federighi, Via del Moro and Via de' Fossi not far from the Piazza degli Ottaviani. The torrent poured into the Borgo Ognissanti and through all the side-streets, spreading to Palazzuolo and Via del Prato, where it met another flow coming through the gate, bringing yet more terror and destruction to the city.

On the left bank of the Arno the flood entered, as stated above, by the Porta San Niccolò and the Via dei Renai and occupied that area as far as the Piazza de' Mozzi. Not being able to spread to the left because of the San Giorgio hill and being unable to continue in its course on account of the rising ground, the water grew steadily deeper in the low-lying parts, and the stretch from the above-mentioned piazza along the Via de' Bardi to the Palazzo Capponi remained unaffected. But from that point the waters rejected by the drains and cellars near the Ponte Vecchio began pouring down the Borgo San Iacopo and the Fondaccio di Santo Spirito to the Porta San Frediano. Though this was the main course of those waters, they also spread up the Via Maggio to near the Sdrucciolo de' Pitti, along the Via del Presto to the Borgo Tegolaia, up the Via Serragli, and to the Piazza del Carmine and the Piazza Piattellina; in short, they flooded all the streets leading off the Borgo San Frediano as far as the gate. These, then, were the extreme limits reached by

the flood within the city. And, as a result of the constant heavy rain, the water remained where it was throughout the 3rd and 4th—and even longer in low-lying districts, where the drains were choked and could not carry it away. All the habitations along the perimeter of the flood had their cellars and ground floors damaged by foul water and mud; and many wells of pure and wholesome water were contaminated and ruined by the impurities carried on the flood. In the low-lying parts of the city, which suffered worst from the flood, many houses and palaces not only lost everything they had in their cellars and ground floors, but were also structurally damaged; floorboards were loosened and pushed up, joists were lifted from their sockets, foundations were undermined and weakened by the violent surging of the water. When the flood at last went down, those unfortunate inhabitants who had not had time to transfer their furniture and other possessions to the upper floors found everything so damaged and so defiled by mud that they would have preferred their treasured belongings to be carried away completely rather than reduced to such a condition. How many poor craftsmen uselessly risked their lives wading into their workshops in search of tools and precious equipment, only to find everything thrown into confusion and rendered unusable by the flood! In short, every storehouse and shop and ground floor in the area I have designated above was damaged to a greater or lesser extent by the unexpected invasion of the waters; and it was heart-breaking to see the loss and hardships that had befallen the unfortunate inhabitants, who now had no hope for the future but in divine mercy and the charity of their fellow men. (Though, as we shall see, their faith in such assistance was amply justified).

Meanwhile the flood continued to grow, and all but filled the arches of the Ponte Vecchio. The goldsmiths and jewellers who have their shops on the bridge, (these shops are in part supported by beams and stone buttresses projecting from the main fabric of the bridge), ran in dismay to secure their most valuable items, terrified that at any moment the timber and tree-trunks carried on the flood might, as it were, cut the floor from beneath their feet and precipitate them into the inferno below.

And so, shortly before midday, saddened by the sight of so much suffering and destruction, and harassed by the scenes which my tortured imagination constantly presented to my mind, I decided to accompany an old friend up to the terrace on the top of the cathedral campanile. We found that many others had preceded us there, drawn as we were, no doubt, by a desire to see for themselves the full scope of the disaster. What a deplorable scene met our eyes when we turned to the west! What anguish tore at our hearts as we gazed upon that devastation! That same Arno which, seen from this terrace at happier times, had appeared to me like a ribbon of silver winding its way beneath the morning sun towards the hills round Signa, was now a turbid flood laden with trees, dead animals, furniture, and articles of all kinds which it had snatched from both town and country. It had burst its banks on both sides, submerging the delightful countryside that stretches for many miles beyond the Porta al Prato and the Porta a San Frediano. Castles, charming villas, the humble homes of the poor, populous villages, the main roads to Pistoia and the Valdinievole and Pisa—all were beset, not only by the Arno, but also by that river's tributaries, so that one habitation was cut off from another, and the people could do little or nothing to help themselves or their neighbours. It was as if the Greve, the Bisenzio, the Ombrone, the Elsa, the Pesa and the Era, together with the smaller rivers, were vying with one another to see which could cause the greatest devastation. And as the same causes, given the same conditions, produce the same results, any detailed account of the damage inflicted upon our unhappy country by this flood would be no more than a repetition of similar narratives inspired by the tragic circumstances of past centuries. And, as on so many occasions in the past, Tuscany has not been the only province to suffer the devastation of fertile lands, the flooding of towns and villages and the destruction of bridges and buildings. Like the Arno, many other rivers—among them the Adige, the Po and the Tiber—were swollen by the extraordinary rains and overflowed into the fair provinces through which they pass.

But I will turn now from the tears and suffering of our city and low-lying country districts, (which had once, for their activity and prosperity, been the wonder and the envy of all who saw them), and take comfort in the thought that the cause of our present lamentation had more in common with that of 1589, (as recounted by Ammirato), than the extent of the devastation it brought; for our Royal Family were residing at Poggio a Caiano at the time of this disaster, just as was the Medici court at the time of the other. Ferdinand I, at the sight of the inundated countryside, travelled with but few companions to Florence by way of Prato in order to provide for the worst afflicted and assure the citizens that he was watching over them; and our Leopold II, who loves to be thought of as the father rather than the sovereign of his people, played no less noble a part in our hour of need. On the night of 2nd-3rd November he charitably set aside some of the buildings on the royal estate for the use of distressed families who had fled from the waters into the horror of the night and were imploring sanctuary. The Prince had clothes and food given to these unfortunates, who had lost all that they possessed. Then, realising the straits to which our city must be reduced by the flood, he set out early the following morning, with only a handful of companions, and courageously made his way by boat to Prato. From there, he made his way as quickly as possible to stricken Florence, and in the streets of that city he was able to see with his own eyes the gratitude with which the people received the constant and truly royal care he had for their well-being. And this was evident even though he toured the city most unobtrusively and could be recognised only by the benevolence and words of comfort which he offered to all whom he met. Nor must we omit to praise the paternal zeal of our most vigilant Gonfalonier and the Magistrature. Ably seconded by units of the military, they did everything possible to relieve the lot of the people, gathering together foodstuffs and, by means of rafts and the few boats available, distributing the same to those unfortunate families trapped in their homes and suffering pangs of hunger which they themselves had no way of satisfying.

Having thus, with great humanity, carried out the tasks most immediately arising from the flood, the authorities began, with the subsiding of the waters, to turn their best attention to the health and economy of the city, speeding the work of cleansing streets, warehouses and habitations of the mud and filth remaining therein. And it was labour, not the zeal and determination of the authorities, that was lacking in the task of restoring the city to its original state of order and cleanness. The persistent rain was also a hindrance; continuing for many days, it aroused fears of a second flood, which would indeed have reduced the city to an evil pass. And here was clear proof of the saying that to those in danger the hours seem days and the days seem centuries. Man does what he can, but prodigies of nature are in the hands of the Almighty.

Nevertheless, as I said before, the most needy of our people were justified in the faith they had in the charity of their fellow-citizens and of those foreigners who have made their homes among us. When called upon to aid those who had suffered in the fearful disaster, all gave freely, irrespective of rank or religion, concerned only to serve their fellow-men in the hour of need; and the generous flow of donations and practical help did much to relieve those who, if they had never known wealth and plenty, had worked hard and conscientiously to augment their slender substance and maintain themselves in their modest yet honourable station in life. The pious call was answered also by the towns and communities of the Grand Duchy which had been spared the flood, and they vied with one another in sending help to the capital and the other afflicted areas of the province.

PHOTOGRAPHIC REFERENCES

SANDY ALTNER: 1, 29, 35, 50. RAFFAELLO BENCINI: 25, 26, 49, 54, 55, 56, 57, 58, 60, 62, 63, 67, 74, 79, 82, 88, 89, 90, 91, 94, 95, 96, 99, 100. PIER LUIGI BRUNETTI: 4, 41, 42, 43, 52, 53, 61. VENIERO DE GIORGI: 21, 37, 38, 39, 51, 65, 72, 73, 75, 76, 78, 80. PIER PAOLO DONATI: 27. FOTO LOCCHI: 2, 6. KRACZYNA: 20. MARIO LO-VERGINE: 24, 33, 34, 69, 70, 71, 77, 81, 83, 97, 98. FOTO MATTEI: 64. FRANCO NEN-CINI: 23, 31, 32, 101, 102, 103, 104, 107. FOTO NOVARESE: 44, 59. LIBERTO PE-RUGI: 5, 8, 9, 10, 11, 16, 22, 28, 30, 40, 45, 46, 47, 48, 66, 68, 84, 85, 86, 87, 105, 106. NICOLA RUBINO: 7, 12. DON STEFANI: 19. GIANNI TORTOLI: 3, 93. ASUNCION VACAS: 13, 14, 15, 17, 18, 36.

The flood-damaged "Zincotipia Moderna". Transferred to other premises, with new machinery, a week after the disaster, this plant was used for the illustrations of this book.

Printed and bound by the Officine Grafiche Fratelli Stianti
Sancasciano Val di Pesa